Doreen Hart

# THE ART OF
# EGYPT

## THE TIME OF THE PHARAOHS

### BY IRMGARD WOLDERING

GREYSTONE PRESS/NEW YORK

Translated by Ann E. Keep

Frontispiece: *Ibis, the sacred bird of Thot, God of Wisdom, and Maat, Goddess of Truth and Justice. Gilded wood and bronze. Late Period, 7th-6th centuries B.C. From Tuna el-Gebel, Middle Egypt. Kestner Museum, Hanover. Width 20.5 cm. Cf. p. 220*

FIRST PUBLISHED IN 1963

© 1962/HOLLE VERLAG G.m.b.H., BADEN-BADEN, GERMANY

LIBRARY OF CONGRESS CATALOG CARD NUMBER: 62-20055

MANUFACTURED IN THE UNITED STATES OF AMERICA

# CONTENTS

# LIST OF PLATES

# LIST OF FIGURES

## LIST OF MAPS

Figures and maps drawn by Ernst Ehlers, Hanover

## ACKNOWLEDGMENTS

The following museums and institutions kindly allowed reproduction of the plates on the following pages:

Walters Art Gallery, Baltimore     184, 185, 186

Robert H. Lowie Museum of Anthropology,
University of California, Berkeley     24

Former National Museums, Berlin     111, 132,
134, 135, 224

Museum of Fine Arts, Boston     46, 63, 182

Brooklyn Museum, New York     17, 204

Oriental Institute, Chicago     45

Royal Scottish Museum, Edinburgh     86, 180

Kestner Museum, Hanover     frontispiece, 19,
114, 183, 203, 206, 223

Pelizaeus Museum, Hildesheim     18, 179, 205

Egyptian Museum, Cairo     22, 23, 25, 26, 43,
66, 84, 85, 112, 141, 159, 161, 162

Rijksmuseum van Oudheden, Leyden     65, 87,
139, 142

British Museum, London     91, 131

Metropolitan Museum of Art, New York (Museum Excavations and Rogers Fund, 1930)     64

Metropolitan Museum of Art, New York
(Gift of Edward S. Harkness, 1926)     83

Ashmolean Museum, Oxford     113

Musée du Louvre, Paris     44, 133, 160, 181

The coloured plates on the following pages were kindly supplied by:

Photo Giraudon, Paris     44, 133, 160, 181

Kersting, London     20, 21

W. Schmölz, Cologne     frontispiece, 19, 114,
183, 203, 206, 223

Uni-Dia-Verlag, Grosshesselohe near Munich

25, 66, 88, 91, 92, 93, 94, 131, 134, 137, 140

Foto Wehmeyer, Hildesheim     18, 179, 205

Zentrale Farbbild-Agentur, Heidelberg     22, 26,
43, 84, 89, 112, 138, 141, 159

# THE PRINCIPAL EGYPTIAN GODS

### ENNEAD OF HELIOPOLIS

*Nun:* Personification of the primeval ocean. Father of the Gods. *Or:*

*Atum:* Human guise. The primeval god of Heliopolis, born of himself. Overlapping functions with the god Nun. God of the setting sun.

*Shu:* Human guise. God of Air. Begotten by Atum from himself.

*Tefnut:* Goddess of Moisture.
*Children of Shu and Tefnut:*

*Geb:* Human guise. God of Earth.

*Nut:* In guise of a human being or a cow. Goddess of Heaven. Later also Goddess of Trees.
*Children of Geb and Nut:*

*Osiris:* Human guise, represented in the swathing of a mummy, with his attributes — a scourge and a sceptre. God of Vegetation. In archaic times, a king. Lord of the Realm of the Dead.

*Isis:* Human guise. Consort of Osiris, mother of Horus. The 'magic realms'.

*Seth:* Human or animal guise (so-called Sethian). National god of Upper Egypt in prehistoric times. In the Osiris legend, the hostile brother of Osiris and Horus' adversary over the legacy of Osiris' terrestrial rule.

*Nephthys:* Human guise. Consort of Seth, sister of Isis.
*Sometimes included in the Ennead is the god*

*Horus:* Guise of a falcon: principal god of Lower Egypt in prehistoric times. National god under the Old Kingdom. His personification on earth is the Pharaoh.
Human guise: son of Osiris and Isis. Lord of the terrestrial kingdom of his father Osiris.

### SUN-GODS OF HELIOPOLIS

*Rē:* Falcon-headed sun-god. who crosses the sky in his barque. Personification of the sun at noon.

*Rēhorakhty:* Falcon-headed. Separate form of the sun-god when he appears radiantly in the sky at sunrise and sunset.

*Khepri:* Guise of a beetle (scarab). Personification of the rising sun.

*Atum:* Human guise. Personification of the setting sun.

*Maat:* Human guise. Attribute: a feather. Goddess of Truth and Justice. Daughter of the sun-god Rē.

### THE OGDOAD OF HERMOPOLIS

Male: guise of a frog; female: guise of a snake.

*Nun and Naunet:* the primordial ocean.

*Heh and Hehet:* infinite space.

*Kek and Keket:* darkness.

*Amun and Amaunet:* concealment.

### THE SACRED TRIAD OF MEMPHIS

*Ptah:* Human guise, wrapped in the swathing of a mummy with various sceptres and a close-fitting cap.
The 'Great God of Creation', encompassing and embodying the 'Ogdoad of Hermopolis' and the 'Ennead of Heliopolis'.

*Sekhmet:* Lion-headed, female. Lord of the desert, bad weather and pestilence.

*Nefertem:* Human guise. God of Scent.

### THE SACRED TRIAD OF THEBES

*Amun-Rē:* Human guise: the 'Great King of the Gods' under the New Kingdom.
Animal guise: ram with twisted horns and goose.

*Mut:* Human guise. Consort of Amun-Rē. The name contains the word 'mother'.
Less frequently, guise of a vulture, in emulation of the Upper Egyptian tutelary goddess Nekhbet, also in vulture form.

*Khons:* Human guise. God of the Moon. Identifiable as the child of Amun-Rē and Mut by the lock of hair on the temple.

### AMARNA

*Aton:* the sun's disc, with rays terminating in

hands. The sun-god, who played a prominent part in the Amarna period.

## GODS OF THE FUNERARY CULT

*Thoth:* Ibis-headed. God of the 15th nome in Lower Egypt. God of Wisdom (at the Last Judgment) and of the Moon. Sacred animals: ape and ibis.

*Anubis:* Jackal-headed. God of the 17th nome in Upper Egypt. God of the funerary cult and mummification.

## GODS OF NOMES AND LOCAL DEITIES

*who occasionally enjoyed more far-reaching significance:*

*Apis:* Guise of a bull. God of Memphis. Consulted as an oracle, especially in the Late Period.

*Bastet:* Head of a cat. The cheerful and friendly succourer. Attributes: basket, sistrum, collar, cat. Sacred animal: cat.

*Bes:* Hybrid creature. Tutelary god of the bou-doir.

*Khnum:* Ram-headed God of Creation. Sacred animal: ram.

*Hathor:* Guise of a cow. Like Nut, Goddess of Heaven. Human head with horns of a cow. Goddess of women and trees.

*Heqt:* Guise of toad. Primeval mother of everything in existence.

*Min:* Human guise. God of fertility.

*Nekhbet:* Guise of a vulture. Tutelary goddess of Upper Egypt.

*Nile-god:* Human guise. Portrayed with papyrus plants, lotus buds, and water-jars, as donor of the Nile and thus of fertility.

*Selket:* Guise of a scorpion. Goddess of medicine.

*Sobek:* Guise of a crocodile. Lord of the Nile.

*Thoueris:* Guise of a hippopotamus. Goddess of fertility and women; gives aid in child-birth.

*Uraeus (Uto):* Snake. Tutelary goddess of Lower Egypt. Attribute of gods and kings.

# INTRODUCTION

Although Egyptian art drew the admiration of the ancients, it did not evoke any very great echo in the Western world until the end of the 18th century. It was only then that a lively interest began to be taken in the land of the Nile.

The scholars who accompanied the Napoleonic armies to Egypt in 1798 were the first to investigate the mysterious works of sculpture and inscriptions that they found there, and in so doing laid the foundations for the scientific study of Egyptian culture.

For a long time Egyptian art remained misunderstood by Europeans, since they proceeded from false premisses. To those brought up in the Greek school, the Egyptian treatment of form inevitably seemed rigid and primitive. It was thought to possess the clumsiness appropriate to an early stage of development, when men had not yet succeeded in representing in an organic and lively manner the world they saw about them.

Only in the 19th century, when excavations were begun and an abundance of works reached European museums, did it become clear how inadequate this traditional aesthetic approach was in attempting to appreciate the genius of Egyptian art. The relationship between the viewer and the work of art is no doubt always determined by aesthetic considerations, but it must not be forgotten that the image obtained in this way is bound to be a subjective one.

In order to assess Egyptian art objectively, it is necessary to know something of Egyptian history in pharaonic times, of Egyptian religion, and of the Egyptians' way of life.

When we look at the monuments, sculptures and reliefs that have been preserved, we are at once struck by their magnificent homogeneity in the expression of form — although we have to bear in mind that, the further back a culture lies in time, the stranger its forms appear to us, and the greater is the tendency to see them as possessing a kind of unity. A close examination of the development of Egyptian art styles reveals that transformation and differentiation took place between one epoch and another, so that, for example, it is possible to distinguish clearly a work of the 3rd millennium B.C. from one of the 2nd millennium B.C. or the Late Period.

This account of the chequered path taken by this great culture over the millennia cannot claim to give more than a brief survey of the most essential facts and artistic monuments, owing to the limited amount of space available for the text and illustrations. But it is hoped that it may encourage the reader to study the original works, both in our museums and above all in Egypt itself, and so stimulate deeper understanding of one of the greatest cultures of antiquity.

# I. BASIC ELEMENTS OF EGYPTIAN CULTURE

The development of an advanced culture such as that of Egypt results from the interplay of a wide variety of factors, which are to a great extent rooted in geography and climate. These exercise an influence upon the way of life of the people and the subsequent trend of their spiritual and artistic evolution. Thus in order to understand the unique genius and form of Egyptian art we have to consider the geography of the country and the evidence relating to its earliest inhabitants.

PHYSICAL SETTING

MAPS PP. 235-7

In prehistoric times Egypt bore an aspect very different from the Egypt of today. The climate was predominantly hot and humid. Where there is now desert there were dense forests, stretches of steppe land, and oases with an abundance of fauna.

As the last episode of the Ice Age came to an end in Europe, a climatic change took place in North Africa which produced a gradual desiccation. The inhabitants migrated from the areas that ceased to be fertile and settled along the banks of the Nile, which at that time probably occupied the whole of the present river valley. Later the river cut a deeper channel and the water level gradually sank, leaving barren mountains in the form of terraces along its banks.

The flint implements found here indicate the route which these migrating peoples took on their way to the Nile and enable us to establish the sequence of stages in their cultural development. Finds from the Lower and Middle Palaeolithic resemble those from a contemporary epoch in Western Europe — for at this time Europe and Africa were still connected by an isthmus between Tunisia and southern Italy — whereas those dating from the Upper Palaeolithic resemble those found from the same period in North Africa, southern Spain and Palestine, but are quite different from those discovered in Western Europe.

The Greek historian Herodotus, who visited Egypt in the middle of the 5th century B.C. and wrote a detailed account of the country and its past, rightly refers to Egypt as 'the gift of the Nile'.

*The Nile*

The long fertile Nile valley, which borders directly upon the vast expanses of the desert, offers a favourable environment for human habitation.

Not far from the ancient capital of Memphis (near Cairo) the river divided into seven branches — only two of which are left today — that irrigated the alluvial lands of the Delta. The valley measures more than 800 km from Aswan on the southern border to the Delta. In Upper Egypt it is bounded to the east and west by barren mountains; in Lower Egypt it is broader and has flat sandy desert on both banks.

With the rising of the river, the so-called swelling of the Nile, which commences each year in July, the land is inundated for three months, leaving a fertile deposit of mud brought downstream from the heart of Africa, where the river has its source. After the flood-waters have receded there follows, in the middle of November, the period of the sowing of the crops. The harvest is gathered in April and May.

In Egypt there is very little rainfall, and the importance of the Nile flood can be judged from the accounts of drought and famine whenever the river failed to reach the normal level. This was why, already in early times, the Egyptians used the nilometer to measure the water level.[1]

*Agriculture* The fertility of the soil made possible the development of settled communities. The inhabitants of the Nile valley joined together in common toil so that they might enjoy the fruits of nature.

The flood-waters were carried inland by means of canals, thus making the soil fertile in areas that were not affected by the flood. Dams were built to prevent the water flowing away.

In order to irrigate fields situated at a higher level a simple implement was invented which is still known in Egypt today. It is called a *shaduf*, and consists of a lever pivoted between two uprights. The shorter lever arm has a weight in the form of a lump of clay, while on the end of the longer lever arm there is a piece of rope, from which hangs a bucket made of skin or plaited material. The bucket is filled with water from the river by lowering the longer lever arm. When it is raised the bucket empties into furrows dug between the fields.

The fact that the fields had to be surveyed afresh after each flooding, which effaced the boundaries, soon led to the establishment of a powerful political authority and a clearly-formulated pattern of social organization. It is no accident that 'stretching ropes' and 'hoeing the soil' are among the activities depicted on the oldest monuments. In the earliest times these were the responsibility of the king. The nomadic hunters who settled on the banks of the Nile became peasants who cultivated the land. Barley and wheat, beans and lentils, gourds, leeks and onions are among the products grown in the soil of Lower Egypt. In the oases of the Libyan Desert and along the northern fringe of the Delta there were luxuriant vineyards. Flax provided the raw material for making fabrics and, together with the moringa tree and castor-oil plant, served as a source of oil.

From representations in relief in tombs dating from the 3rd millennium B.C. we may obtain information about the life of the peasants and the implements that were used in agriculture. A wooden plough, usually drawn by horses, served to break up the top-soil; the clods thrown up were cut into small pieces by means of a hoe, and then the crop was sown. At harvest time the corn was cut with a sickle, bound in sheaves, and taken to the threshing-floor by donkey. There it was trodden out by oxen or donkeys, and winnowed again by women. In addition to agriculture an important part was played by livestock-raising. The peasants had cattle, sheep, goats and donkeys, as well as poultry (ducks, geese and pigeons). The donkey served as mount and beast of burden, playing the part which in Greek times was assumed by the camel. *Cattle-raising*

Big game was still to be found in Lower Egypt in the 5th millennium B.C., but was pressed back to the south during the 4th millennium. From hunting scenes we know that there was much more big game in Egypt in antiquity than there is today. In the barren valleys and mountain areas, even in historical times, there were lions, leopards, antelopes, gazelles, ibexes, jackals, giraffes, ostriches, and other species — only few of which are still to be met with in Egypt today. The hunting of big game with bow and arrow was one of the favourite pastimes of the king and his nobles in historical times. Like the trapping of birds and harpooning, it is frequently depicted on shrouds. By means of skiffs made of bundles of papyrus stems tied together, it was possible to penetrate into the marshy jungle, and to hunt aquatic birds with throw-sticks, or to kill fish, or even hippopotamuses, with harpoons or two-pronged spears. Hunting was soon followed by trapping birds and fish in clap-nets and trawl-nets. The latter were particularly popular among the peasantry. *Hunting* *Fig. 31* *Plate p. 91*

There were few trees, although more than are to be found nowadays. Sycamore, acacia, tamarisk, honey-locust, moringa, date-palm and doum-palm are among the trees that provide shade from the sun's rays. Already in early times the Egyptians used to regard them as the abodes of gods. Timber was so scarce that it had to be imported from *Trees*

the Lebanon. Egypt has just as little in the way of mineral resources. In the eastern desert, in the area of the present-day Wadi Hammamat, gold was found in small quantities. The amount available was much greater in neighbouring Nubia, which from the 3rd millennium onwards was under Egyptian sovereignty.

The exploitation of the Nubian gold deposits provided the wherewithal for the rapid development of the goldsmiths' craft. Silver, too, was only available in small quantities on Egyptian soil. It was imported from Asia Minor, especially during the period when Egypt was the leading world power. Copper, which already at an early date supersedes flint as the material used for implements, was obtained from mines in the Sinai Peninsula. The popular turquoise also originates from that area. There is evidence of the use of bronze, an alloy of copper and tin, only from the Middle Kingdom onwards.

The scarcity of wood and metals is offset by the existence of various kinds of stone. These furnished material for temples and statues, of which so many have survived from all periods of Egyptian history. In the mountain ranges bordering on the Nile valley to the east and west there are different varieties of limestone. The most suitable for buildings, and especially for reliefs, was the fine white limestone quarried near Tura, in the area of the ancient capital of Memphis.

In Upper Egypt, in the district of Edfu, and in particular near Gebel Silsila, a fine-grained sandstone was quarried, which was particularly favoured in the New Kingdom for statues and sarcophagi. Not far from Aswan, in the south of Upper Egypt near the First Cataract, where a granite barrier blocked the course of the Nile, black and red granite was quarried. It was used by Egyptians in all periods of their history, and was frequently transported for great distances down the Nile. Near Mallawi in Middle Egypt there were stone quarries which yielded a yellowish-white alabaster. In the area of the ancient desert route leading from Coptos to the Red Sea there was black and green basalt, breccia and porphyry. This area, nowadays called the Wadi Hammamat, was particularly rich. It also yielded semi-precious stones such as rock crystal and cornelian.

The transport of metals and stone — not all the quarries were situated directly along the Nile — was often an arduous task. Expeditions had to be sent to procure the precious material, which were obliged to work under very difficult conditions. This is clear from the inscriptions they left behind at the sites.

In spite of the significance of the Nile, which is the life-line connect-

16

PLATE 1 — Small female figure of painted clay. Funerary gift. Prehistoric Period, 4th millennium B.C. From Mamarija. *Brooklyn Museum, New York. Height 29 cm. Cf. p. 32.*

PLATE 2 — Painted clay vessel featuring flamingos and ibexes. Prehistoric Period, Nagada II, close of 4th millennium B.C. *Pelizaeus Museum, Hildesheim. Height 21.5 cm. Cf. p. 33.*

PLATE 3 — Vessel of speckled breccia. Archaic Period, approx. 2800-2660 B.C. *Kestner Museum, Hanover,*
*Height 17.5 cm. Cf. p. 33.*

PLATE 4 — View of step pyramid of King Zoser at Sakkara. Old Kingdom, IIIrd Dynasty, approx. 2660-2590 B.C. *Cf. p. 68*.

PLATE 5 — Sphinx of King Chephren, with the Pyramids of Giza to the rear. Limestone. Old Kingdom, IVth Dynasty, approx. 2500 B.C. *Cf. p. 72.*

PLATE 6 — False door from the tomb of Ateti at Sakkara. Painted limestone. VIth Dynasty, approx. 2320-2160 B.C. *Egyptian Museum, Cairo. Cf. p. 75.*

PLATE 7 — Geese: detail of frieze painted on plaster. From the tomb of Atet at Meidum. Old Kingdom, IVth Dynasty, approx. 2725 B.C. *Egyptian Museum, Cairo. Cf. p. 8 o.*

PLATE 8 — Painted limestone relief showing Wepemnofret at table. The inscription gives his titles, name and other offering gifts. Old Kingdom, IVth Dynasty, approx. 2550 B.C. From Giza. *Robert H. Lowie Museum of Anthropology, University of California, Berkeley. Width 66 cm. Cf. p. 81.*

PLATE 9 — Diorite statue of King Chephren. The divine Horus falcon, whose earthly incarnation is the pharaoh, is shown protecting the king's head with its wings. From Giza. Old Kingdom, IVth Dynasty, approx. 2500 B.C. *Egyptian Museum, Cairo. Total height 1.68 m. Cf. p. 100.*

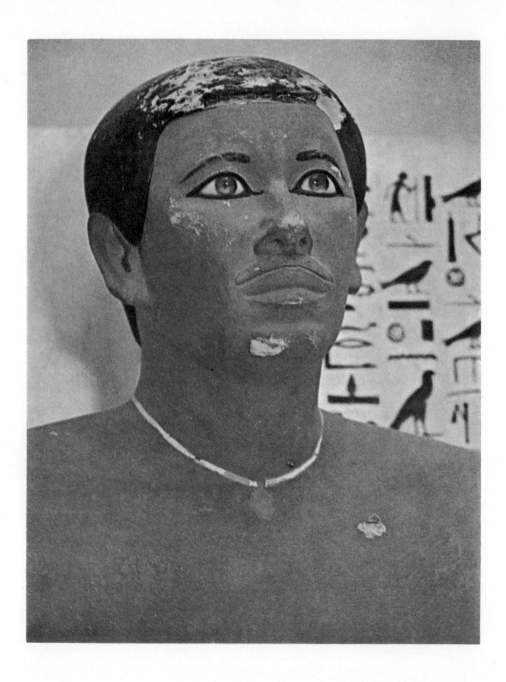

PLATE 10 — Painted limestone statue of Prince Rahotep, son of Snefru. From Meidum. Old Kingdom, IVth Dynasty, approx. 2580 B.C. *Egyptian Museum, Cairo. Total height 1.20 m. Cf. p. 101.*

ing north and south, Lower and Upper Egypt are quite distinct from a topographical point of view. In Upper Egypt the river valley is only a few miles wide and is bordered by sheer barren mountains. In Lower Egypt it is broad and eventually merges into the Delta. In this flat and fertile valley, adjoined by sand dunes, with the expanse of blue sky above, the physical environment was quite different from the south. So, too, was the way of life of the inhabitants. In Lower Egypt agriculture and livestock-raising led to the formation of an agrarian society of settled communities, whereas in Upper Egypt men continued to live as nomadic shepherds and hunters. Here men were slower to develop a sense of nationhood, since nomads do not have a firm attachment to the soil. Their life is less regimented and much harder than that of the peasants, but it is also more vigorous and independent. Lower Egypt, and the Delta area in particular, were throughout Egyptian history open to external influences, whereas Upper Egypt, on the other hand, remained almost untouched by them. This helps to explain the leading part played by the former area in the country's political and cultural development.

The sharp distinction between the two parts of the country is also reflected in the use of the term 'the Two Lands'. Lower and Upper Egypt have their own individual plant symbols or standards (papyrus and sedge) and tutelary deities (Horus and Seth). The king, who holds sway over both parts of the country, wears the Egyptian Double Crown, comprising the crowns of Lower and Upper Egypt.

*'The Two Lands'*

The contrast in the course of development of the two areas is due to ethnic as well as to physical differences. The Upper Egyptian nomads of the 5th and 4th millennia B.C. belong to the Hamitic tribes of Africa, who must be regarded as the original indigenous population. It is, however, an open question whether, and to what extent, they comprised older elements that had been absorbed. On the other hand, the agricultural population of Lower Egypt is definitely of a different origin, and also less homogeneous, than the Hamites of Upper Egypt. Racial links are more probable with Palestine and Syria than with African groups.

*Ethnic composition*

These differences in the ethnic composition of the population in Egypt are corroborated by philological as well as anthropological evidence. The construction of sentences, vocabulary, and phonetics in Egyptian suggest links with West African, North African and Hamitic languages as well as with the Semitic languages spoken in Palestine, Syria and Asia Minor.

In the life of the Egyptian people religion plays a far more important part than modern man can imagine.

With the peoples of antiquity, as in Europe in the Middle Ages, belief in gods or in one god forms the focal point of man's world-outlook. Religion provides the stimulus to art and philosophy, and a matrix for the development of moral principles. Religion establishes the relationship between man and a superior being not subject to earthly laws. We commonly use the term 'religion' to denote an outlook based on a revelation (a gospel) containing commandments regulating human conduct. Belief in revelation and the interpretation of the commandments by priests lead to the formation of an organized community of believers, which mediates between the individual and the divinity. To the religious man God appears in a form comprehensible to his imagination and His commandments teach him to distinguish between good and evil. By humiliating himself man feels a sense of security, in that he enjoys divine protection. In God's laws he possesses an infallible guide by which to shape his conduct.

In Egypt there is no generally binding gospel, no revelation.

The cosmic view of prehistoric man is characterized by a unity between the individual ego and the world at large. Man is not as yet cognizant of any distinction between his personal being and the world about him. He does not distinguish between earthly and supernatural phenomena.

Prehistoric man, not yet conscious of himself as an individual, and having no sense of space or time, regarded the phenomenal world as alive with magic forces.

In the Neolithic period the formation of groups, tribes and districts may have led to a gradual growth of consciousness, which subsequently dissolved his bond with the world of nature and enabled him to distinguish between the real and the supernatural, between life and death.

*Fetish* Nature — plants and stones as well as animals — is conceived by prehistoric man as imbued with supernatural magic power. He venerates it as a fetish, i.e. as a reflection of the eternal forces, and represents the image of the deity in the form of fetishistic sacred signs, which are thought to afford protection and ward off evil. In Egypt some of these have been handed down to us in the emblems representing individual districts (nomes).

*'Divine Animals'* The most important of the phenomena that are imbued with magic

power are animals. They played a major part in the life of Egyptian peasants and shepherds, who both valued them and feared them. As 'divine animals' the crocodile, snake, falcon, vulture, cow and others were given the function of intermediaries between man and the supernatural forces. As the nomadic tribes became settled these became local deities, and special places of worship were established for them.

On the other hand, the veneration of great natural cosmic forces, manifest in the sun, moon and stars, as well as in the Nile flood, was not linked to any particular place of ritual. This later gave an impetus to the development of myths and religious systems which in historical times led to the formation of a religious cosmic concept (concept of the universe). *Cosmic forces*

The relationship between man and these beings imbued with divine power is one of veneration and magic invocation. Attempts were made to influence them by ritual acts, pictorial representations, and magic incantations. This fundamentally magical outlook is later overlaid by other concepts, but is never eradicated entirely and remains alive in popular beliefs. It permeates the attitude to life and religious outlook of the Egyptians until the decline of ancient Egyptian culture. *Magic*

For as far back as we can trace it, the Egyptians believed in survival of the dead in another world. In Egypt, as in no other country, men's deeds and thoughts were governed by concern for the after-life. Their settlements, cities and royal palaces, built of very impermanent material, have fallen into ruin, and only a few traces of them are left. But the royal mortuary temples and the lavish tombs of princes and courtiers testify even today to men's hopes of eternal life.

Most of what is known about the life of the ancient Egyptians – about their actions as well as their ideas – is derived from representations in their tombs, funerary gifts and inscriptions.

In the Delta and in Lower Egypt the dead were interred inside the settlement, in their own houses. Since they remained in close relationship with the living they did not need any funerary gifts. When — towards the end of the 4th millennium in particular — the dead began to be buried outside their settlements, their tombs were given the shape of houses. In Upper Egypt the dead were buried away from the settlements in oval-shaped pits, together with a number of funerary gifts.

# II. THE PREHISTORIC ERA

The prehistoric era comprises the period from the 5th to the 3rd millennia B.C. Most of the settlements have been buried under layers of mud deposited by the Nile during the intervening centuries.

MAP P. 237

Only on the western border of the Delta, not far from Merimde, in the Faiyum, and at several places in Upper Egypt have traces of settlements been authenticated. Excavations have shown that in prehistoric times stone architecture was completely lacking. For their dwellings men built simple huts of reeds or lumps of clay, round or oval-shaped in plan, caulked on the inside with rush-matting.

*Finds* The flint implements found — adzes, spear- and arrow-heads — show skilful workmanship. Bone needles and awls were used for working skins. Remains of plaited baskets and woven materials show that these manufactures were also known.

*Tasa* The pottery found in Neolithic settlements bears geometric ornamentation. At Tasa, Upper Egypt, ornaments are incised and fill-
*Merimde* ed in with white paste. At Merimde, Lower Egypt, burnished red clay vessels have a herring-bone pattern all the way round them below the brim, while burnished black pottery has an ornamental strip along the brim consisting of rows of lines or dots.

Attempts at sculpture in the round are not known from the Neolithic period. Their absence is related to the fact that in prehistoric times man had not yet developed a sense of ego-identity: he was not conscious of himself or the phenomenal world, and for this reason was not concerned with representing it artistically.

*4th millennium* At the beginning of the 4th millennium B.C. the use of copper
*B.C.* brings about an important turning-point in the development of man's technical abilities. At first copper is to be found as jewellery, in the form of small bars or beads, but it was not long before implements and weapons of copper were made. They had far greater possibilities than flint implements both as weapons and as tools for use by peasants and artisans.

*Badarian culture* Finds from the Stone and Copper Age (Chalcolithic period), made predominantly in Upper Egypt, are known as the Badarian culture after the chief site, Badari in Upper Egypt. These products can also be identified in Nubia and as far away as the area of the Red Sea.

FIG. 1 — *Ivory female figure. Funerary gift. From Badari. Prehistoric Period, Badarian culture, approx. 4000 B.C. British Museum. Height 14 cm. Cf. below*

Badarian culture is characterized by burnished red clay vessels with a black brim (produced by oxidization) and by clay and bone figures sculptured in the round representing animals and human beings. Small ivory female figures are shown with deep eye-sockets, a broad mouth, and a large hook-nose. The breasts and pudic triangle are accentuated. The arms are detached from the body and the legs are splayed.

Badarian culture is superseded by Nagada culture, named after the site of Nagada in Upper Egypt. It is divided into two phases, clearly distinct from one another, termed Nagada I and Nagada II. Painted Nagada I pottery, which originated from Upper Egypt, was made of burnished red clay and painted white and yellow. In addition to ornaments in the shape of triangles, lines arranged in a herring-bone pattern, and stellar designs, there also occur representations of animals and human beings. Where figures are rendered they are mostly indicated by lines, while the body is suggested by lattice-like inner markings. Occasionally a plastically-carved animal figure is attached to the exterior or brim of the vessel. In the case of scenic compositions featuring figures, these are for the most part hunting scenes in which one may perceive the connection between the actions of the individual figures.

So far as the technique of painting is concerned, the treatment is still austere, two-dimensional and ornamental, but the picture obtains an intrinsic value and no longer serves a secondary purpose as decoration on pottery, as was the case with the finds from Merimde, Tasa and Badari.

In addition to painted clay vessels stone ones occur for the first time. They are made of basalt and are hemispherical and squat in form.

*Nagada I*

FIG. 2

FIG. 2 — *Vessel of red burnished clay with white decoration. Funerary gift. Prehistoric period. Nagada I, 4th millennium B.C. Musées Royaux du Cinquantenaire, Brussels. Height 29 cm. Cf. above*

31

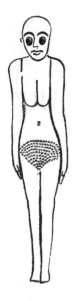

FIG. 3 — *Female figure. Funerary gift. Prehistoric Period, Nagada I, 4th millennium B.C. From the MacGregor Collection, present whereabouts unknown. Cf. below*

Among Nagada I bone carvings a prominent place is occupied by thin pillar-like female figures with high arcs suggesting eyebrows and circular eye-sockets. The nose and lips usually exhibit elaborate workmanship. The arms rest upon the body and the legs are placed close together. A different group comprises male statuettes of slender build with narrow oval-shaped heads and large protruding ears. The arms hang down and are frequently detached from the body.

When carving bone it is not so easy to treat figures with full plasticity owing to the technical difficulties involved, whereas soft clay is easily modelled. Clay sculpture, although cruder and more perfunctory than carvings on bone, has yielded a rich variety of motifs. Thus for the first time attempts are made to represent man in relation to his environment or at work. One small clay sculpture shows men in a boat; another represents a man brewing beer in a vat. [2]

Representations of animals — hippopotamuses, cattle or baboons — testify to a keen sense of observation. They reproduce in an appropriate fashion the characteristics of each species. The instructive variety of clay sculpture had no influence upon the stylistic development of monumental sculpture in historical times. It died out almost completely in the Archaic Period. But the austerity manifest in the bone carvings, on the other hand, foreshadowed the way in which form was expressed in the 3rd millennium B.C. Clay vessels from the Nagada II culture, which originated from Lower Egypt, may be clearly distinguished from the ware in use prior to that period. They are modelled from a yellowish-grey or reddish-brown unburnished clay, and are painted in a brilliant red. Among the ornaments that are still favourites nowadays pride of place is taken by wavy lines and spirals. Among the figures that frequently occur are boats rowed by several oarsmen, with cabins and standards, animals of the chase such as the gazelle, antelope and flamingo, and female dancers with their arms raised above their heads. Unlike the custom in the preceding period, when the body was depicted ornamentally, resolved down

PLATE P. 17

*Nagada II*

to lattice-like designs, it is now represented as a plane, painted in a PLATE P. 18 bright reddish-brown colour.

The figures show no sign of being composed to form definite scenes. The only wall-painting which has survived from the late prehistoric period originates from Hierakonpolis. The ground is painted yellow over a black area round the base. The colours of the individual figures are black, white and reddish-brown. They show boats as well as hunting and battle scenes, arranged arbitrarily. The sparse fragments housed in the Cairo Museum, which must serve as a substitute for the two-dimensional compositions that have not survived, correspond from the standpoint of theme and technique to the painted clay vessels from the Nagada II culture.

In the latter half of the 4th millennium B.C. stone receptacles were produced as well as clay vessels. They were made with the aid of a bow-drill, a tool that became known at this time. The chief material used was the gaily-coloured breccia found in the Wadi Hammamat. PLATE P. 19 The importance attached to the discovery of the bow-drill can also be seen from the fact that later it was chosen in hieroglyphic writing as the sign for a craftsman.

The painted clay vessels from Nagada I and II reached an apogee of perfection that was never attained later in this technique. Clay vessels were soon ousted by receptacles made of stone, metal or faience. They were used almost exclusively as storage vessels and utensils, and for this reason remained barren of any decoration.

Little in the way of sculpture has survived from the Nagada II culture. Two small human figures, worked in stone for the first time, still show considerable rigidity. 3

Prehistoric sculpture was definitely not based on the idea of creating works that would strike the viewer as an artistic expression of the world in which he lived. The stimulus to the production of sculpture was the magic function which the small figures had to fulfil. They were placed in the graves of deceased persons. The Egyptians believed that they would protect the dead from danger and assure them pleasures of every kind in the world beyond. They conjure up a magic and supernatural reality.

Whereas Badarian culture was probably diffused over the whole of Africa, Nagada I culture is limited to Egypt, Nubia and the adjoining desert areas. But Nagada II culture centres on Upper and Lower Egypt. It is superseded directly by the Egyptian culture of historic times. The variety of sculptured figures in the prehistoric era may in some ways point to the beginnings of an advanced culture, but we do not find any features that herald classical Egyptian style, either as regards its spiritual basis or its principles of artistic form. The great turning-point, in art as in all other fields, comes with the transition to the Archaic Period.

WRITING From monuments erected at the turn of the 4th and 3rd millennia B.C. it may be deduced that at this time the whole country was united under Upper Egyptian hegemony.

The simultaneous discovery of hieroglyphic writing and the introduction of a calendar show that there was an awakening historical consciousness which prepared the way for the development of a high culture in Egypt.

*Hieroglyphs* The hieroglyphic writing discovered at the beginning of the Ist Dynasty, which had developed into a fully perfected system by the end of the IInd Dynasty, reproduces in its symbols men, animals, plants and objects, but is not simply a system of pictorial representation of actual objects (pictographs). Only a few hieroglyphic symbols, called determinatives or ideographic signs, possess no phonetic value, but follow a word simply as an ideogram in order to explain its meaning. Thus to denote action a striking arm was added, or a proper name would be accompanied by the picture of a seated man or woman. Most of the hieroglyphs, however, possess phonetic values which have nothing to do with the meaning of the picture. The development may be seen as having taken place as follows: originally a word was reproduced by means of an ideogram, but later words of the same phonetic character which did not have the same meaning as the picture were expressed by the same hieroglyphic symbol.

It is all the more probable that hieroglyphs should have been used for words that sounded similar, because in Egyptian script vowels and endings were not indicated. As in other Oriental scripts, such as Hebrew or Arabic, only the consonants were written down. We have therefore no more than a vague idea of the spoken language and the way in which it was pronounced. This simple system subsequently underwent a further stage of development in that words which consisted of only one consonant and one vowel were used as symbols for one consonant, or as letters.

In this way all the consonants came to be represented by symbols. It is surprising that in spite of all this the Egyptians should not have hit upon the idea of using the 24 signs representing single consonants as an alphabet. Signs representing two or more consonants as well as determinatives were retained throughout as well as letters. It was left to the Phoenicians in the 13th century B.C. to produce an alphabet consisting of consonants, which was to become the basis of purely alphabetic writing.

Hieroglyphic writing was the script found on monuments, the walls of tombs and temples, the plinths of statues and supporting back-pillars, and on funerary stelae. The Greeks called the Egyptian signs *hieroglyphoi:* 'carved sacred symbols'.

*Hieratic script*

In addition to hieroglyphic writing a cursive script was developed for everyday use. It was employed for setting down religious texts, judicial decisions, literary tales, or even letters. This 'hieratic script' is derived from hieroglyphs, but the original ideograms can hardly be recognized in their abbreviated form. Writing was performed with the aid of a reed, frayed at the tip like a brush. The papyrus plant provided the writing material: wafers were obtained from the pith of the plant and laid at right angles on top of one another, and then beaten to form a thin sheet, cut, whereupon several pages were pasted together to form a standard roll. At first writing was in vertical columns, but from the time of the Middle Kingdom onwards in horizontal lines from right to left. For short notes potsherds or flakes of limestone, known as *ostraca,* were used instead of papyrus (whence our word 'paper' is derived).

*Demotic script*

In the Late Period, approx. from the 7th century onwards, an even more abbreviated derivative of hieroglyphic script was used for official documents. This 'demotic' script consisted almost entirely of lines. Up to the 3rd century A.D. all three varieties of writing were in use: hieroglyphs as the script on stone monuments; hieratic for long manuscripts written on papyrus; and demotic for official documents. At the beginning of the 2nd century A.D. the Egyptian language began to be written down in Greek letters, which resulted in vowels being indicated as well. This mode of writing was used by the Coptic Christians, especially in setting down the lives of the Coptic-Egyptian church fathers. Coptic is of particular significance to us since many valuable conclusions may be drawn from it with regard to vowels that have not been handed down in hieroglyphic writing.

*Coptic script*

During the later phases of antiquity, when knowledge of the Egyptian language had been lost, Greek scholars studied the hieroglyphs and explained that this must be a symbolic script, in which magic secrets were concealed. The evaluation of Egyptian art, religion and language by the Greeks, who attached the greatest importance to the

*Deciphering of hieroglyphs*

mysterious and secret aspects of every manifestation of Egyptian art, was no doubt one of the factors why scholarly interest in the land on the Nile was only awakened at such a late epoch. At the beginning of the 17th century the key to the Coptic language was rediscovered, but it was not until the beginning of the 19th century that the hieroglyphs could be deciphered. Earlier attempts in this direction, particularly those of the Jesuit scholar Athanasius Kirchner, who studied the obelisks in Rome, failed because it was assumed that the script was purely symbolic and pictorial. The attempts at interpretation that have been recorded led to the weirdest results.

The stimulus to the deciphering of the hieroglyphs was given by Napoleon's expedition to Egypt in 1798, in the course of which a stele was found not far from the town of Rosetta, on the Mediterranean coast. This Rosetta Stone bears an inscription in Greek, demotic and hieroglyphic writing, and contains a decree from the year 196 B.C. summarizing the benefactions conferred by Ptolemy V upon the priesthood. It was written by the priests of Memphis and is now in the British Museum.

While studying the hieroglyphic inscription on the Rosetta Stone it became evident that two groups of words were written inside ovals (cartouches). The conjecture that these were proper names was subsequently confirmed. It was from this idea that the brilliant French scholar Champollion set out in his investigations. Although he, too, at first regarded the hieroglyphic writing as a symbolic one, he assumed that the proper names of Ptolemy and Cleopatra, which appeared in the Greek text, must also be reproduced in the hieroglyphs as recognizable letters. He did indeed discover, in the hieroglyphic writing inside a cartouche, identical signs in lieu of the consonants 'p', 't' and 'l' which are common to both the Greek names. By comparing them with other names in cartouches on ancient Egyptian monuments, it could be ascertained that the Egyptians must also have used alphabetic signs. After more than ten years of work, in the course of which he made further comparisons with Egyptian inscriptions, aided by his knowledge of Coptic, Champollion succeeded in deciphering hieroglyphic writing and elucidating the system on which it was based. His work was carried on by a number of European scholars, and during the 19th century hieratic and demotic writing were deciphered as well.

Hieroglyphs, which are seldom absent from monuments dating from historical times, have since become one of the most important sources of information about events in ancient Egypt, as well as the religious beliefs and everyday life of the Egyptians. The pictorial signs express so well the original prototype — the idea of the object they represent — that when they were invented they could be used to denote concepts. They almost invariably fuse with the matter to which they relate in such a way as to form a harmonious whole. Thus it is barely possible to distinguish between the picture and the writing. This applies particularly to the great ornamental inscriptions of the Middle Kingdom.

Just as the discovery of writing is an indication of man's awakening sense of the need to communicate, to hand on to posterity information about events of historical or general importance, so also this new historical consciousness leads him to discover a means of setting down the concept of time. To establish chronological divisions it was natural in an agricultural country such as Egypt for men to take as their starting-point the inundation season of the Nile, because this occurred fairly regularly and determined the pattern of farming during the year. Thus when the Nile begins to rise the New Year — the Nile Year — commences as well. Irregularities in the rise of the river may have led to attempts to find a more reliable means of establishing the beginning of the year. The solution was found in the heliacal rising of the star Sirius, which the Egyptians called Sothis and venerated as a goddess. At dawn on a certain day — July 17th, according to our calendar — Sothis re-appeared for the first time in the year. The annual heliacal rising of Sothis (Sothic rising) coincided roughly with the beginning of the inundation season of the Nile, and for this reason was fixed as the commencement of the New Year.

The year was divided into three seasons of four months, each of thirty days, to which five extra (intercalary) days were added. This schematic calendar of 365 days was invariable. Since it was a quarter of a day shorter than the Nile Year, there was an ever-widening gap between New Year's Day and the beginning of the Nile Year. This error amounted to one day every four years, which of course affected not only New Year's Day but also the festivals connected with sowing and harvesting. Had an extra day been inserted every leap year, these difficulties would have been overcome, but this was not done until the Julian calendar was introduced by Julius Caesar in 46 B.C. As a result of this growing anomaly, 1461 Egyptian calendar years correspond to 1460 Sothic periods and the same number of Julian solar years. After every 1460 years the commencement of the Nile inundation period coincides exactly with New Year's Day according to the Sothic rising.

Egyptian texts contained astronomical data referring to the Sothic rising, the so-called Sothic dates which, owing to the schematic nature of the Egyptian calendar, can be used for chronological purposes. Thus, for example, a papyrus from Illahun, now in Berlin, records the rising of Sothis in the 7th year of the reign of King Sesostris II (XIIth Dynasty) and the medical 'Papyrus Ebers' a rising of Sothis in the 9th year of the reign of Amenophis I (XVIIIth Dynasty). With the aid of some dates relating to the new moons in the same papyrus we can work out that the Sothic rising in the reign of Sesostris II took place in the year 1872 B.C.

*Written sources* In addition to these astronomical data we also have a number of other important sources at our disposal which can help us to follow the course of Egyptian history. Inscriptions on the walls of temples and tombs, finds of papyri, archaeological material, and finally the accounts of ancient travellers — all these sources provide material for historical research.

During the Ist Dynasty the year was named after some special event, recorded on small ivory tablets. Later the collection of taxes, approximately every other year, served as a basis for chronological computation. From the Middle Kingdom onwards the chronology was based upon the year of the king's reign, each reign commencing with the Year 1. The Egyptians never introduced a system of continuous chronology.

For the events of the Old Kingdom we have the Palermo Stone, which records the succession of rulers from the beginning of the Ist Dynasty to the Vth Dynasty. There are detailed lists of kings engraved on the walls of the temples of Thutmosis III at Karnak and Seti I at Abydos. The Turin Museum houses the famous Royal Papyrus from the period of Ramses II, which contains a list of all the rulers between the Ist Dynasty and the New Kingdom.

A document of equivalent significance is the history written in Greek by Manetho, an Egyptian priest, in the middle of the 3rd century B.C. The original has unfortunately perished, and we know it only from fragments handed down by Josephus and Julius Africanus. Thanks to the lists of kings we have an almost complete record of Egyptian rulers, from the first king of the Ist Dynasty — Menes — to Alexander the Great. In the case of a number of kings we also know the years of their reign. This gives us a fairly firm framework for classifying

Egyptian history by periods. We can also draw upon astronomical data and parallels with Near Eastern chronology, as well as information yielded by the comparative study of archaeology.

The grouping of the Egyptian rulers into 30 different reigning houses (dynasties) was made already by the priest Manetho, and was then adopted by Egyptologists. The latter also divided Egyptian history into longer periods, which they termed the Old, Middle and New Kingdoms and the Late Period.

# III. THE ARCHAIC PERIOD

HISTORICAL SURVEY

Egyptian history begins with the unification of the kingdom by King Menes, who brought the whole country under the control of Upper Egypt and founded the Ist Dynasty in or about 2950 B.C. His name has been recorded by the historian Herodotus and in the lists of kings from the New Kingdom, but there is no reference to him on the Palermo Stone from the Vth Dynasty.

No sooner have we embarked upon the study of Egyptian history than we are faced with the problem of deducing historical facts from records and archaeological finds. Our conclusions can often be no more than tentative.

The royal titulary in Egypt consists of five distinct elements and was fully developed by the end of the Old Kingdom. The king's favourite title was 'Horus', which indicated that he was a personification of the god of that name. The second title is derived from the two heraldic animals of Lower and Upper Egypt, the snake and the vulture, known as *nebty* ('the Two Ladies'). The third royal title describes the king as 'strong bull', the fourth as 'son of the sun-god Rē', while the fifth name refers to him as king of Lower and Upper Egypt, using the symbols of the heraldic plants of the two lands — the papyrus and the sedge. This last title is followed by the proper name of the king. The first pharaoh in Egyptian history, Menes, has two other names that have been recorded. Among the monuments from the close of the 3rd millennium there was discovered a cosmetic palette of King Narmer, wearing the Crown of Lower as well as that of Upper Egypt. This leads to the supposition that he was the king who united the 'Two Lands'. But there are also a few finds bearing the name of King Hor Aha, which show a stylistic affinity with the Narmer palette. The initial syllable of his name, Hor, suggests that in the name Hor Aha we have the Horus name of the first pharaoh. Hor Aha must have held sway over the whole country, as is clear from the fact that small writing tablets occur featuring double inscriptions relating to Lower and Upper Egypt. Thus we have the two heraldic plants and the two heraldic animals. On another small tablet we find side by side the Horus name Aha and the *nebty* name Menes, which may perhaps mean that Menes was the second title of the king whose Horus title was

FIG. 6

Aha and whose personal name may perhaps have been Narmer. Greek tradition has it that Menes, the unifier of the kingdom, originated from the town of This in Upper Egypt, and for this reason the term Thinites was introduced with reference to kings of the Ist and IInd Dynasties. Herodotus states that Menes founded the town of Memphis, surrounded it with a white wall, and built a sanctuary in honour of the god Ptah. The sacred bull, Apis, is also known to have been worshipped as early as the Ist Dynasty.

*Thinites*
*Ist and IInd*
*Dynasties*

Little has been recorded about specific historical events from this time. Campaigns were undertaken against the Beduin tribes in the Sinai peninsula, which opened up access to the malachite found in that area. Sinai was for thousands of years the main source of this important raw material, essential in the production of copper. The new state also had to assert itself in battles against the Libyans in the west and the Nubians in the south.

MAP P. 235

The ruler of the united Egyptian kingdom not only derives his right to govern from the gods but is himself the human incarnation of the falcon god Horus.

*Monarchy*

The belief that the king is identical with the god Horus served to enhance the prestige and authority of the pharaoh among the subjugated tribes of Lower Egypt, for the divinity of the king is a guarantee of law and order. The lives and well-being of his subjects depend on him. He understands the language of the gods; as a powerful figure, he can deal with the mighty on their own terms.

The sovereign emblem — the cone-shaped White Crown of Upper Egypt, the cap-like Red Crown of Lower Egypt, and the whisk and sceptre — are all thought to be charged with magic force.

A corollary of man's awakening consciousness in the Archaic Period is the desire to honour the divine powers, not only in the form of fetishes or animals, but also by creating an image of the deity. Thus develops the concept of gods as beings with animal heads and human bodies.

RELIGION

The ancient belief in the magic power of animals is now combined with the view that the gods act in a manner comprehensible to the human imagination. The features of the animal-god (jackal, falcon, snake or crocodile) are transferred to the god in half-human, half-animal form. They give the latter his particular characteristics and determine the functions he performs, which are appropriate to his nature. Men use their imagination to obtain more lifelike and human concepts of the qualities of their gods. They are given a sanc-

FIG. 78 tuary in a certain district or town. Deities connected with the laws of the cosmos, such as Min, Osiris, Ptah and Khons, are represented in the form of idols, in human shape but swathed like mummies. In the same way divine standards and sacred symbols are provided with human arms, which indicate their efficacy.

It is obvious that observation of the process of growth and decay in nature, the sequence of seasons and other phenomena, should impress upon men the inevitability of their eventual death. The Egyptians came to see death as the result of divine intervention. In the figure of Osiris they worshipped the mysterious power that gives the soil its fertility and watches over the cycle of death and re-birth.

*After-life* Life in the world beyond is seen as corresponding to that in this world. Even in the 'Goodly West', where (as is suggested by the setting sun) the land of the dead is thought to be situated, men must till the fields and carry on their daily tasks. For this reason dishes of food are placed into their tombs to provide the necessary nourishment. Weapons, implements and servant figurines are intended to facilitate the work of the deceased in the world beyond. There he should also be provided with cosmetic palettes, jewellery, and all that goes to make life pleasant. These objects, or even the portrayal of them on the walls of the tomb, are thought to be imbued with magic force. A flint knife placed in the grave has to be carefully broken lest it should fall into the hands of some enemy and prove useful to him. For the deceased person it is a magic aid. A clay servant figurine may have deformed arms and legs, or alternatively his arms may be tied to his back, in order to prevent him rebelling against the authority of the deceased or running away. In spite of this mutilation belief in the magic power of the image ensures that it will perform its function as a servant.

The thorough care taken for the after-life stems from a feeling of insecurity and from fear of the mysterious eternal powers, to which man feels that he is subject. He distrusts the gods and seeks to intimidate them by making use of esoteric knowledge and magic forces. This is the way in which, in the Pyramid texts, the divine power of the king is solicited against that of the gods:

' "There is strife in heaven, we see a new thing [the deceased king]" say they, the primordial gods.

The Ennead of Horus is dazzled, the Lords of Forms are in terror of him.

He [the deceased] seizeth the sky, he cleaveth its metal [of which the

PLATE 11 Painted limestone statue of Princess Nofret, consort of Prince Rahotep. From Meidum. Old Kingdom, IVth Dynasty, approx. 2550 B.C. *Egyptian Museum, Cairo. Total height 1.18 m. Cf. p. 101.*

PLATE 12 — Painted limestone statuette of Kay, a judge and nomarch. Found in his tomb at Sakkara. Old Kingdom, Vth Dynasty, approx. 2400 B.C. *Louvre, Paris. Height 53 cm. Cf. p. 103* .

PLATE 13 — Limestone statuette of potter. Funerary gift. Old Kingdom, early VIth Dynasty, approx. 2200 B.C. *Oriental Institute, Chicago. Height 13.3 cm. Cf. p. 104.*

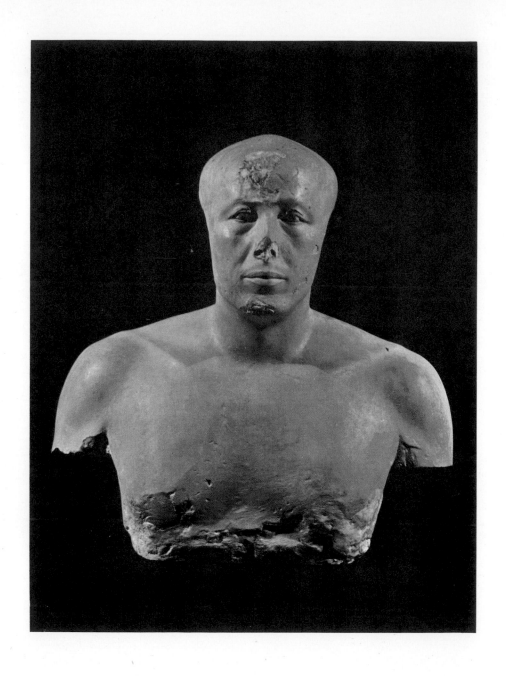

PLATE 14 — Bust of Prince Ankh-haf. Limestone, covered with stucco and painted. From his tomb at Giza. Old Kingdom, IVth Dynasty, approx. 2480 B.C. *Museum of Fine Arts, Boston. Height 50.6 cm. Cf. p. 102.*

sky is formed]. He setteth alive in the west, the dwellers in the nether world follow him, and he riseth renewed in the east.

He that adjudged the quarrel [Thoth, god of wisdom] cometh to him, making obeisance. The gods are afraid of him, for he is older than the Great One. He it is that hath power over his seat. He layeth hold on Command [the decision taken by the rulers], Eternity is brought to him. Discernment is placed for him at his feet.

Cry aloud to him in joy, he hath captured the horizon. His glory is in the sky, his power in the horizon like Atum his father that begat him — he begat him but he is stronger than he. He is the Great Mighty One that hath power over the mighty ones. His duration is eternity and his boundary everlastingness.' 4

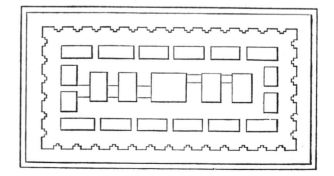

FIG. 4 — *Ground-plan of tomb at Nagada. Ist Dynasty, approx. 2900 B.C. There are five chambers in the interior of the superstructure, which serve as the sarcophagus-chamber and for the storage of supplies and funerary gifts for the deceased. They are enclosed within a wall broken by projections and recesses. Principal example of a type of tomb otherwise found only in Lower Egypt. Cf. p. 48.*

# IV. TOMBS AND ARCHAEOLOGICAL FINDS FROM THE ARCHAIC PERIOD

At the beginning of historical times, when the nomadic tribes of Upper Egypt had become settled and Egypt had built up a state organization headed by a king, the need was felt to enhance the monarch's prestige and support his sovereign claims by building palaces. In the same way temples were erected for the worship of the gods. From the tent of the Upper Egyptian nomads there developed a palace similar in form to a tent; and the typical Lower Egyptian dwelling, made of bricks of mud from the Nile, became a monumental structure, in the form of a dwelling, with a vaulted roof and enclosed by a wall broken by projections and recesses.

*Burial places*

*Lower Egypt*

The architecture of burial-places developed along different lines in the two parts of the country. In Lower Egypt, towards the end of prehistoric times, the rectangular pit was lined with bricks of Nile mud and divided into sections by small walls. These ancillary chambers served to accommodate funerary gifts. With the beginning of the Ist Dynasty the tombs become larger and are furnished with a vaulted brick roof and occasionally a flight of steps at the entrance. To indicate the site of the tomb above ground a low rectangular brick structure with retaining walls is erected.

*Upper Egypt*

The royal tombs of the Ist and IInd Dynasties discovered near Abydos in Upper Egypt are at first no more than simple pits, but they soon develop into spacious burial-places. They are furnished with recesses for funerary gifts and ancillary chambers for the interment of members of the royal court, and also have flights of steps. King Wedimu had his burial-chamber lined with granite slabs. King Khasekhemiu, last king of the IInd Dynasty, had at his disposal a sepulchral chamber dressed with limestone slabs. The superstructures of the Abydos tombs have unfortunately been so badly damaged that we cannot obtain an accurate idea of their appearance. There is, however, evidence to suggest that a mound of sand was piled on the grave, held in place by a brick retaining wall. The burial-place was indicated by an offering-table and two tall stelae bearing the name of the king, in front of which the funerary rites were conducted.

*Nagada tomb*

FIG. 4

In contrast to these burial-places in Upper Egypt, another type of tomb has been discovered, predominantly in Lower Egypt, which has a brick structure above ground in the shape of a large rectangle, the four wall faces of which are broken by projections and recesses. In the interior there are five chambers, of which the one in the centre served as a sarcophagus chamber. The others were used for keeping funerary gifts and food supplies. The ceiling of the tomb consisted of trunks of palm-trees.

Of this type of tomb, found as a rule only in Lower Egypt, one specimen, better preserved than any other, was discovered at Nagada in Upper Egypt. The material used almost exclusively for monuments during the early period was brick made of clay.

Archaeological finds from the Archaic Period provide an insight into the important developments that took place in the field of art and at the same time enable us to draw conclusions with regard to political events at the time of the establishment of the Old Kingdom. Students of history have found particularly valuable the slate cosmetic palettes, used for grinding eye-paint already in prehistoric times. From the first Nagada culture onwards animal figures were occasionally carved on these slate palettes, which were at first lozenge-shaped. A little later there occur, as well as lozenge-shaped and round cosmetic palettes, others in the shape of animals, the edges of which were worked to form birds' heads, fish-fins or horns. Finally, a change was brought about by carving ornamental designs in relief on the palette itself. The original purpose of the palettes gradually faded into the background, and the whole palette was furnished with figures in relief on

ARCHAEO-
LOGICAL
FINDS

*Cosmetic palettes*

Fig. 5 — *Battle-field palette. Late Prehistoric Period, approx. 3000 B.C. Slate. Battle-field with corpses and carrion vultures. The lion probably symbolizes the victorious king. Above: captives being marched off by two standards with human hands. British Museum and Ashmolean Museum, Oxford. Cf. p. 50.*

FIG. 6 — *Slate cosmetic palette of King Narmer. From Hierakonpolis. Beginning of Ist Dynasty, approx. 2950 B.C. King Narmer, wearing the Crown of Upper Egypt, is striking one of his defeated enemies with his club. The divine Horus falcon is bringing a symbol of the subjugated Land of Papyrus, the Delta. Above, right and left: head of the goddess Hathor, in the form of a cow, with Narmer's name inscribed in between. This motif became a formula for rendering the triumphant pharaoh. Identical examples are found in Egypt even as late as the period of Roman rule. Egyptian Museum, Cairo. Height 64 cm. Cf. pp. 40, 51.*

both sides. These ceremonial palettes play an important part in the development of reliefs in Egyptian art. The most successful of them, in which there is most harmony between the different parts, may be assigned to the Ist Dynasty, since it bears the name of King Narmer. FIG. 5 The 'battle-field palette', which still belongs to late prehistoric times, represents a lion tearing to pieces one of several corpses strewn over a battle-field. The lion must be regarded as a symbol of the king. Vultures and ravens are depicted hovering around the spot. In the upper register captives are being marched away by two standards furnished with human arms. Unfortunately, the battle-field palette is not complete. It is therefore impossible to decipher the two hieroglyphs that give the name of the enemy country, which are set over the head of the lion, since they have been preserved only in a fragmentary condition. It nevertheless appears probable that this scene portrays a historical event which the Egyptians, with their newly-awakened historical awareness, regarded it as worth while to record. The character of the scene and the style are still clearly pre-historic, whereas the well-known Narmer palette opens up a new world in which a formal rigidity of structure is the rule. The obverse side, with the depression for grinding eye-paint, is divided into three registers. On top we can see the king triumphing over his Lower Egyptian enemies. He is wearing the Crown of Lower Egypt. In the middle, framing the depression, are two creatures with sinuous necks, part lion and part snake. Below this the king, portrayed as a bull, is breaking down the wall of an enemy stronghold. On top the palette terminates on either side in two heads of the goddess Hathor. She is

represented with cow's ears and horns, between which is set the name of King Narmer.

The reverse side is almost completely taken up by a composition used until the most recent period of Egyptian art to symbolize a victorious FIG. 6 pharaoh: the king, wearing the Crown of Upper Egypt, has seized by a tuft of hair an enemy who has collapsed before him, and is preparing to strike him with a mace. Over this enemy is an explanatory sign, 'harpoon district'. Above, on the right, a falcon is depicted with a human arm, leading along like a prisoner the subjugated 'land of papyrus' (the Delta). The two scenes relate to historical events connected with the unification of the 'Two Lands' — Lower and Upper Egypt.

The other figures disposed in an arbitrary fashion over the battlefield palette are here arranged in proper order on the plane, which is divided into several zones. This disposition, and manner of relating the figures to one another, constitute a step towards the development of the style adopted in Egyptian reliefs: the variety and abundance found in the early pictures are here subjected to formal principles. The tectonic arrangement of the plane gives the entire composition clarity and restraint. The rigid structure is also evident in the handling of individual figures, which have a tendency towards solidity. As befits its importance, the principal figure is larger than the subsidiary ones — a principle kept to in later Egyptian art. This corresponds to the inclination of Egyptian artists, who do not follow their visual impressions when representing a figure, but instead seek to convey the significance of a subject by portraying it in an abstract manner, outside space and time. The breaking up of the plane into zones, and the introduction of base lines on which the figures are placed, constitute one of the main principles of arrangement in Egyptian reliefs. The unique character of Egyptian art is from now on unmistakable. Comparable to the historical scenes on cosmetic palettes are others depicted on mace-heads and on ivory knife-handles.

*Relief carvings*

At the beginning of the Ist Dynasty relief carvings on bone and ivory also developed rapidly in the direction of a classical style. Attempts have on occasion been made to explain this swift progress as due to the influence of Mesopotamian art. Several motifs, such as that of the antithetic group, have undoubtedly been borrowed from Mesopotamia — for example, the bone knife-handle from Gebel el-Arak. [5] The relief on this shows a man, wearing a long tunic and a turban-like cap, between two lions, completely identical in form, which are springing at him from the left and from the right.

The influence of Mesopotamia on the development of Egyptian art was not, however, of very great significance. During the centuries that followed there are also only a few examples of such influence. It was only with some hesitation that stone was used as a material for

*Reliefs on stone*
FIG. 7

reliefs. As well as reliefs on stone vases and mace-heads, we have funerary stelae from the Archaic Period, most of which only have a few engraved symbols of names and titles. These tall rectangular slabs, which are frequently round-topped, were sunk vertically into the ground. Towards the end of the Ist Dynasty a figure of the deceased was sometimes added, as well as his name and title. Most of the stelae known from this era come from Abydos in Upper Egypt, where they were erected in the vicinity of royal tombs.

In Lower Egypt, in the area of Memphis, on the other hand, there were discovered rectangular horizontal plaques showing the deceased at the dining-table — a motif which was later to become an accepted canon in the pictures in funerary temples.

The penultimate king of the Ist Dynasty, Semerkhet, had himself portrayed on a rock-face in Sinai as a victorious pharaoh triumphant over his enemies, in the same fashion as on the Narmer palette. This is the oldest known monumental stone relief in Egyptian art. [6]

*Sculpture*

The reliefs carved on bone and ivory are related to a number of ivory statuettes found at Hierakonpolis, in Upper Egypt. Those that have survived from prehistoric times are mainly small plastic female figures, but from the Archaic Period we have a preponderance of statuettes of gods and private persons. This ivory sculpture, apparently originating from the first half of the Ist Dynasty, shows amazing harmony in the treatment of the body and the detailed modelling of the face. The manner of rendering the garment and cloak on some of the figures suggests that they were intended to represent reality, as well as being magic symbols. Whereas the clay and ivory figures from prehistoric times had no base and were simply placed in the grave (or into the sand), the sculptured figures from the Archaic Period had a base. They could thus be placed erect, and given a more pronounced three-dimensional quality. The base makes the figure a work of sculpture in its own right.

As well as the finds at Hierakonpolis there are a number of statuettes, mostly depicting a woman with a child, which are meticulously modelled, and carry on the tradition of the much cruder clay sculpture of the prehistoric era.

Copper and faience were also used as material for small sculptured figures, but it was not long before larger statues came to be made of stone. This was available in large quantities in the country and was best suited to the tendency towards monumentality that is characteristic of Egyptian art.

So far as animal figures are concerned, the hippopotamus and lion, which in prehistoric times were represented as wild and fearsome beasts of prey, with jaws wide open, are now (early 3rd millennium B.C.) rendered with majesty, restrained buoyancy, and energy. Their dangerous and savage nature, liable to show itself at any time, is checked by strict formal laws, thereby raising them to the level of works of art.

Among carved animal figures there are some masterpieces of realism which contrast with the crudity and clumsiness of the earliest figures of deities in human guise. Three statues of the god Min from Coptos, larger than life-size, do not anticipate in any way the spirit of classical Egyptian art: the cylinder-shaped body is almost unarticulated, and they resemble pillar-like idols. [7]

The few specimens there are of large-scale human figures in the round, most of them depicted in a seated or squatting posture, also show inexperience in the treatment of proportion and lack of uniformity in composition. Not before the appearance of two statues representing King Khasekhemui of the IInd Dynasty do we glimpse FIG. 8 the beginnings of the development that was to reach its climax in the sculpture of the Pyramid Period. The king, wrapped in a cloak and wearing the Crown of Upper Egypt, is seated upon a cube-shaped stool with a low back support. His right hand, with fist clenched, rests upon his right thigh, and his left hand on his right forearm. The form is compact, evoking a sense of austere dignity. The convention for depicting the human figure has been established. With only slight modifications it was to govern the treatment of Egyptian statues in the round for thousands of years to come.

The great political and religious changes that occurred at the beginning of the historical era, and the consequences that flowed from them, provide the answer to our question as to the purpose and significance of stone sculpture in this period. The humanization of the gods led to the erection of temples and places of worship. The new concepts of what life was like for the dead in the world beyond necessitated the construction of well-equipped burial-places modelled on the houses of the living. The position of the god-king had become one of overwhelming importance in political and religious life. These factors resulted in the production of cult figures and statues of the god-king, which were erected in temples and soon in funerary temples as well. Important dignitaries may also have enjoyed the right to have statues of themselves erected in the temple, close to that of the king, as his servants and worshippers. Whether these were funerary figures, such as we find in tombs of courtiers from the IIIrd Dynasty onwards, cannot be ascertained, since no funerary figures have been found either at Sakkara or at Abydos.

FIG. 8 — *Statue of King Khasekhemui, wearing the Crown of Upper Egypt and a long cloak. Green stone. From Hierakonpolis. Late IInd Dynasty, approx. 2600 B.C. Egyptian Museum, Cairo. Height 56 cm. Cf. p. 53.*

# V. THE OLD KINGDOM

The reign of King Zoser, first ruler of the IIIrd Dynasty, marks the beginning of the period of the Old Kingdom. Its capital was at Memphis, in Lower Egypt, which became the focal point of the economic and cultural life of the country.

HISTORICAL SURVEY

*IIIrd Dynasty*

During this era Lower Nubia, situated to the south of the First Cataract, came under Egyptian rule for the first time. Of the successors of King Zoser there is hardly any record; it seems that for a time the united kingdom once again became divided among them.

MAPS PP. 235-7

The transition from the IIIrd to the IVth Dynasty was apparently the result of the marriage between Queen Hetep-heres and Snefru, who was thereby enabled to claim the throne. He became the founder of the IVth Dynasty. During his reign, it is recorded, a campaign was undertaken against Nubia and an expedition sent to Byblos to obtain cedar-wood. Reliefs found in Sinai provide information regarding the efforts made to exploit the mines in this area. The names of his successors on the throne of the pharaohs — Cheops, Chephren and Mycerinus — have become immortal through the construction of the great Pyramids at Giza.

*IVth Dynasty*

The annals of the kingdom give an account of the campaigns undertaken against the Lybians and Nubians and record the erection of strongholds, dams and temples. This sparse information scarcely does justice to the power and splendour attained by the Egyptian kingdom at this time. Fortunately, enough monuments have survived, such as pyramids, temples, tombs, sculptures and reliefs, for us to obtain some idea of the spirit that animated the Pyramid Period.

The transition from the IVth to the Vth Dynasty came about through Queen Khent-kaus' marriage to Userkaf, who secured the throne. At the beginning of the new period great changes took place in the outlook of the people, which weakened the absolute power of the sacrosanct king.

*Vth Dynasty*

During the VIth Dynasty, especially during the reign of Pepi II, the decline in the central monarchical power becomes clearly evident. His reign is traditionally said to have lasted for 90 years, and is described in literary sources as an age of decline, social revolution and internecine strife. After the death of the last king of the VIth

*VIth Dynasty*

Dynasty chaos arose. The political and social order was disrupted. Authority and law were called into question. The royal pyramids were ransacked, tombs and statues destroyed. The prevailing insecurity and unrest are apparent from literary texts which give a trenchant picture of the conditions that existed in the country. One prophet, for example, utters the following warning:

'Nay, but plunderers are everywhere.
Nay, but poor men now possess fine things.
He who once made for himself no sandals now possesseth riches.

Nay, but the high-born are full of lamentations,
And the poor are full of joy. Every town saith:
"Let us drive out the powerful from our midst".

Nay, but laughter hath perished and is no longer made.
It is grief that walketh through the land, mingled with lamentations.

Nay, but that hath perished which was still seen yesterday.
The land is left over to its weariness, as when one hath pulled up the flax.

Would that there might be an end of men

. . . but the land turneth round as doth a potter's wheel'. 8

*VIIth-Xth Dynasties*  Several kings belonging to the VIIth and VIIIth Dynasties figure in the lists of kings, with only short reigns. They were rulers who attempted to found new dynasties at a time when the state power had disintegrated.

While revolution raged in Lower Egypt, the princes of Coptos and Abydos succeeded in gaining control over parts of Upper Egypt. But only the nomarchs of Herakleopolis, who had property in Middle Egypt, are accounted reigning pharaohs. They are listed as kings of the IXth and Xth Dynasties. The founder of the IXth Dynasty, the nomarch Kheti, chose the ancient capital of Memphis as the seat of his government. He held sway over Lower and Upper Egypt, whereas in the nome of Thebes local princes obtained power and then gradually extended their rule northwards. The conflicts between the nomarchs of Herakleopolis and those of Thebes have been recorded in inscriptions on the tombs of nomarchs at El Bersha and Asyut, in central Upper Egypt. After the collapse of the Herakleopolitan dynasty, brought about by the Theban prince Mentuhotep II in or about 2040 B.C., Egypt was once again united under one sovereign. Mentuhotep II is listed as the first king of the XIth Dynasty — the Middle Kingdom.

In the IVth Dynasty the absolute power of the god-king, who was called the 'Great God', extended over the religious life of his people as well. The pharaoh was seen as linked by a personal bond to the gods. It is he who provides his courtiers with a burial-place not far from his own tomb (pyramid) and grants offerings for funerary rites. In inscriptions on tombs one continually finds the formula: 'an offering given by the king'. The deceased is referred to as 'honoured by the Great God'.

Only in the inscriptions on royal monuments is information given about men's relations with their gods and their hopes in regard to the world beyond.

As the organization of the state expanded during the course of Old Kingdom history, there was a growing tendency to share governmental responsibility, offices, privileges and prestige. This decentralization of political power led to the development of the nomes, and the crystallization of a bureaucracy that gained increasingly in importance.

The religious concepts of this period were no longer restricted to veneration of a god-king and magic invocation of deities in the guise of human beings, animals, or hybrid forms. As men acquired a greater degree of consciousness, they became more inquisitive about the secrets of nature: about the origin and development of the earth, and the laws governing the movements of the stars. Cosmic forces came to be venerated as deities. The Egyptians imagined them in human shape, or as hybrid beings with human bodies and animal heads. These cosmic deities were thought to have created the world and to control its destiny. They were universal deities, whose activities were not linked to any specific place of worship. Fanciful myths and speculations led to the development of various religious systems which considered the problem of the origins of the world and of life itself.

*Cosmic deities*

According to the doctrine of Heliopolis the principal deity is Atum, who created himself. He begat Shu, god of air, and his female counterpart Tefnut, who in turn brought forth Geb (earth) and Nut (sky). They had four children: Osiris, Isis, Seth and Nephthys. The

*Doctrine of Heliopolis*

Heliopolis pantheon consists of the 'sacred ennead'. As father of the gods the place of Atum is occasionally taken by Nun, the personification of the chaotic primordial ocean from which a mound of earth rose up — the Earth, which is subordinate to the earth-god, Geb. He is associated with his spouse Nut, the sky-goddess, who is depicted as a woman or a cow. Her body forms the horizon, over which the falcon-headed sun-god, Rē, sails in his barque. The sun is venerated in three guises: as a scarab, or sacred beetle (*kheper*, 'to come into existence'), when it rises in the morning; at noon it appears as the falcon-headed god Rē; and in the evening it takes human shape as Atum. Each morning the sky-goddess Nut gives birth to the sun-god, and he begins his journey across the sky from east to west, while Shu, god of the air, affords protection to the sky-goddess, who stands over the recumbent earth-god Geb.

The king had hitherto been 'Great God', as a manifestation of the divine power of the Horus falcon. Under the influence of the doctrine of Heliopolis he became the son of the sun-god, Rē. He is no longer identical with the god Horus, but obtains legitimation as a descendant of the sun-god. The latter is represented in human shape with a falcon's head, and thus in form resembles the ancient national god Horus. The term 'son of Rē' is incorporated into the royal titulary. Almost all the rulers of the Vth Dynasty have the syllable Rē as part of their names.

The weakening of the king's claims to divinity reflected the change that took place in political life and the new relationship that existed between man and the gods. In early times the Egyptian faced his deities in a spirit of fear: he knew nothing of their character, and was therefore only able to approach them by means of magic invocations. In the sun-cult nature and man both have their place in the great cosmic process; each has its meaningful part to play. This belief removes some of the terror attaching to the world beyond and lends a note of near-gaiety to men's world-outlook during the Vth Dynasty.

*Doctrine of Hermopolis*    A different doctrine, that of Hermopolis in Middle Egypt, explains the origin of the world in terms of eight elemental forces (ogdoad); Nun, the primordial ocean, and his female counterpart Naunet; Heh, the infinite space, and Hehet; Kek, darkness, and Keket; Amun, 'the hidden (god)', and Amaunet. They represent the original state of the cosmic order. The four pairs of concepts are made manifest as primeval beings which have risen out of the mud: the males are depicted as frogs and the females as snakes. As in the Heliopolis doctrine a primeval mound emerges from the waters, and on it the sun-god rises out of an egg. With his appearance the cosmic order is created.

In the town of Memphis, the capital of Egypt during the Old Kingdom period, men worshipped the god Ptah, who appeared in human guise. In the theology of Memphis the eight primeval gods of Hermopolis, who played a part in the creation of the world, are combined in the person of the god Ptah, while the ennead of gods at Heliopolis are regarded simply as manifestations of Ptah. Ptah is the god of creation, and as the deity of the capital he is superior to all the other gods. He carries out the act of creation with 'his heart and tongue', i.e. by his 'thought' and by 'utterance'. He knows the nature and name of all things, and by mentioning them gives them life — a concept that is in complete accordance with the magic beliefs current among the Egyptians. Knowledge of the name and familiarity with certain sayings confers superiority and power.

*Doctrine of Memphis*

The theology of Heliopolis, with its veneration of the sun-god Rē, left its mark upon later religious thought in Egypt. When the sun set in the west in the evening, men asked themselves what course it took until it rose next morning. The Egyptians believed in the existence of an introvert sky inhabited by demons, where various dangers lurked. Men may have soon come to relate their own lives to the journey taken by the sun across the sky during the day and its disappearance from view during the night. They will have wondered what was to become of them after death, and have been anxious to traverse the skies in the barque of the sun-god, and to help him ward off spirits and demons when he passed through the nether regions.

*Concept of the after-life*

Alternatively, men entertained the hope of an after life in the 'Field of Rushes' in the east, where the sun-god Rē used to bathe, where the fields were as fertile and rich as they were nowhere else — a land where no man knew want or suffering.

The ideas held about the world beyond varied greatly. As well as desiring to traverse the sky in the sun-barque, or to live in the 'Field of Rushes', men believed in a realm of the dead among the circumpolar stars, 'stars which never set'. The ancient belief in a land of the dead in the 'Goodly West' also survived. In addition to these concepts, according to which the world beyond was to be found outside the limits of the terrestrial world, there was a belief that the deceased lived on in his tomb — his 'eternal house'.

From literary sources, as well as from a representation from New Kingdom times in the Mortuary Temple of Hatshepsut, it appears

FIG. 42

that the Egyptians believed in an immortal spiritual substance which they called *ka*. In the scene showing the divine birth of Hatshepsut the ram-god Khnum is depicted in the act of shaping, on a potter's wheel, the royal child. The latter appears twice in the same guise. One of the figures can be identified as *ka* by the hieroglyphic sign showing two upraised arms. During a man's lifetime his *ka* is contained within him, but after his death it is set free, and takes up its abode in his funerary statue, which is erected in the statue-chamber *(serdab)* of his tomb. During the burial service the priest performs the rite of 'opening the mouth' on the statue, touching its lips with a special implement to ensure that it accepts the *ka* — the immortal soul of the deceased. The concept of *ka* was at first associated only with the king, but later it was extended to all men. It ensured them eternal life in the tomb, which was now also referred to as 'the House of Ka'. Prayers for the dead, and formulae uttered when making sacrificial offerings, are addressed to the *ka* of the deceased.

The unrest and disorder that prevailed between the Old and Middle Kingdom periods had a shattering effect upon the entire mode of thought of the Egyptians. Literary texts contain expressions of resignation and despair — as, for example, in the following lines:

'To whom do I speak today?
Brothers are evil,
Friends of today, they are not lovable.

To whom do I speak today?
Men are covetous,
Every one seizeth his neighbour's goods.

To whom do I speak today?
Gentleness hath perished,
Insolence hath come to all men.

To whom do I speak today?
He that hath a contented countenance is bad,
Good is disregarded in every place.

To whom do I speak today?
Faces are invisible,
Every man hath his face downcast against his brethren.

To whom do I speak today?
Hearts are covetous,
The man on whom men rely, hath no heart.

To whom do I speak today?
There are none that are righteous,
The earth is given over to the workers of iniquity.

To whom do I speak today?
I am laden with misery,
And lack a trusty friend.

To whom do I speak today?
The sin that smiteth the land,
It hath no end.' 9

Despair and scepticism with regard to a blissful existence in the world
beyond also result in increased emphasis being laid upon this world,
as can be seen from the following song of a harpist:

'Bodies pass away and others remain
Since the time of them that were before.
The gods that were aforetime rest in their pyramids.

What are their habitations?
Their walls are destroyed,
their habitations are no more,
as if they had never been.

None cometh from thence that he may tell us how they fare,
that he may tell us what they need,
that he may set our heart at rest,
until we also go to the place whither they are gone.

Spend the day happily and weary not thereof!
Lo, none can take his goods with him.
Lo, none that hath departed can come again.'10

The belief in the divinity of the pharaoh had been shattered. Hitherto men had entered into contact with the gods through the medium

of the god-king, who represented the whole nation. Now it was seen as the task of each man to establish contact with the gods for him-himself. Responsibility passed to the individual. The attitude to the world beyond also changed: all terrestrial matters are now said to be transitory, and man yields to this fate. In the dispute between a man tired of life and his soul we are told:

'Death is before me today
As when a sick man becometh whole,
As when one walketh abroad after sickness.

Death is before me today
As the odour of myrrh,
As when one sitteth under the sail on a windy day.

Death is before me today
As the odour of lotus flowers,
As when one sitteth on the shore of drunkenness.

Death is before me today
As a well-trodden path,
As when a man returneth from the war unto his house.

Death is before me today
As when a man longeth to see his house again,
After he hath spent many years in captivity.' 11

*Osiris myth*  Out of the doubts, fears and chaos that prevailed during this era there developed an ethos that presupposed the existence of a just god, who judged men by their deeds, not by their possessions or their worldly power. The new outlook was no longer compatible with the cheerful and consoling sun-cult of the Vth Dynasty. The ancient god of vegetation, Osiris, was revived and elevated to prominence. According to the Osiris myth, recorded in Egyptian and Greek sources, Osiris is a king who ruled in prehistoric times. His brother Seth begrudges him his power, and the two brothers begin to fight. Seth murders his brother and throws his body into the sea. Isis, his lamenting spouse, finds Osiris' body, which a crocodile had carried on its back to the shore. She prays to the gods, utters sacred formulae, anoints his body, and by waving her wings restores to him the breath of life. Thus Osiris

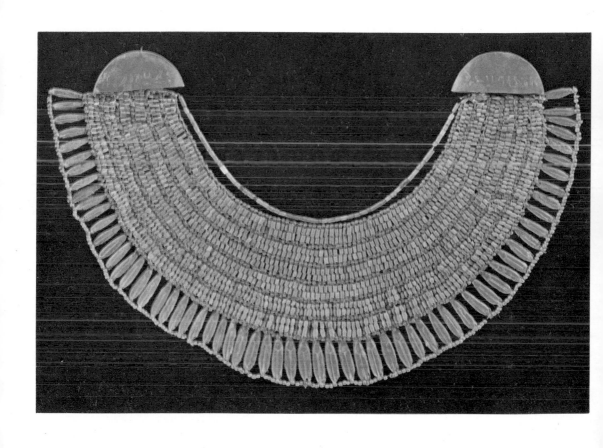

PLATE 15 — Gold collar necklace from the tomb of Impy. Old Kingdom, VIth Dynasty, approx. 2200 B.C. *Museum of Fine Arts, Boston. Length 27.5 cm. Cf. 104.*

PLATE 16 — Detail of papyrus showing the Last Judgment, presided over by the god Osiris, ruler of the realm of the dead. The jackal-headed god Anubis is depicted weighing the heart of the deceased, in his absence (in the left-hand scale of the balance) against the sign for truth and justice (in the right-hand scale). From the tomb of a female musician of the god Amun at Deir el-Bahari. XXIst Dynasty, 1185-950 B.C. *Metropolitan Museum, New York. Cf. p. 108.*

PLATE 17 — Painted limestone relief. Tombstone of Khui, from Abydos. Middle Kingdom, XIIth Dynasty, 1991-1785 B.C. *Rijksmuseum van Oudheden, Leyden. 37 x 61 cm. Cf. p. 124.*

PLATE 18 — Sphinx of Amenemhat III. Black and green hard rock. From Tanis. Middle Kingdom, XIIth Dynasty, 1842-1795 B.C. *Egyptian Museum, Cairo. Length 2.25 m. Cf. p. 126.*

is resurrected. In the court of the gods he withstands the accusations of Seth, is found to be 'true of speech', and is awarded the dignity of ruler over the realm of the dead. His son Horus, after a long dispute before the divine court, is appointed to succeed his father Osiris and to hold sway over the earth.

Like Osiris, man was also destined to die and to rise from the dead to a new life in the world beyond. The Osiris legend thus became the symbol of the fate of mankind: at death man became an Osiris. This belief provided Egyptian religion with a new profundity which was to bear fruitful results, especially in the Middle Kingdom period.

# VI. ART AND ARCHITECTURE IN
# THE OLD KINGDOM

ARCHITECTURE Nothing expresses to such effect the austere monumentality and time-lessness of Egyptian art as the Pyramids. They have been for thousands of years the hallmark of ancient Egypt.

After the unpretentious beginnings made in the Archaic Period, the sudden appearance of monumental stone architecture represents a tremendous achievement, both from the technical point of view and with regard to the spirit in which the Pyramids were erected. The step pyramid at Sakkara,[12] built by the brilliant architect Imhotep *Zoser Pyramid* as a sepulchral monument to King Zoser, is an expression of the god-PLATE P. 20 king's new claim to supreme power. The sequence of rooms and architectural elements corresponds to that in the royal residence at Memphis — for this is indeed a residence, designed for life in the world beyond. The buildings of the terrestrial palace, of brick and other perishable materials — the entrance hall, coronation hall, cer-FIG. 9 emonial pavilion, and the administrative buildings behind the great rectangular enclosure wall — are here translated into stone in the form of dummy buildings, so that they may be of eternal service to the royal household in the after-life.

Evidence of the merging of ideas held in Upper and Lower Egypt is provided by the use of the Upper Egyptian concept of a sepulchral monument, as in this pyramid, and the Lower Egyptian tradition of designing the tomb in the form of a house. The result is this reproduction of the terrestrial residence of the ruler. Some details of the layout also reveal Lower Egyptian as well as Upper Egyptian architectural ideas.

In the enclosure wall of the pyramid area there are 14 two-leaved false doors. The actual access to the whole complex is through a huge gate in the southern part of the eastern side, which leads to an entrance hall some 54 metres in length. Light penetrates through apertures in the wall above.

This long room is divided into niches by 20 tongue-walls which run from the longitudinal walls on both sides to a passage-way in the centre. They terminate in columns imitating clusters of plants. The ceiling reproduces the form of round tree-trunks. Adjoining the entrance hall is a large court with a massive simulated structure in the south-western corner. This is a tomb with underground burial-chambers. Like the burial-chambers to be found inside the step mastaba, they are lined with green faience tiles which simulate the reed-matting formerly used to decorate internal walls.

The purpose of these burial-chambers still remains unclear. It has been suggested that the fact that there are two of them is designed to represent the duality of the 'Two Lands', Upper and Lower Egypt, in a manner similar to that found in the royal titulary, plant emblems, and elsewhere. The actual royal tomb was situated underneath the pyramid.

Another court with various buildings round it may be identified as a ceremonial court similar to that in the residence. It was here that ceremonies were performed in connection with the great royal jubilee. Pictorial representations of these festivities and the record of a dramatic performance which probably took place at the time of the king's accession show that the royal jubilee was one of the most important ceremonies in the Egyptian calendar. It is therefore understandable that the residence built for the after-life should be furnished with the buildings necessary for its celebration.

In the smaller courts there are two dummy buildings, which may be administrative buildings of the 'Two Lands'. Next to the one in the north, in front of the wall, there are three papyrus columns, perhaps symbolizing the Lower Egyptian heraldic emblem, the papyrus. In these the plant is represented in a stylized form, but one can still

FIG. 9 — *Tomb complex of King Zoser at Sakkara. IIIrd Dynasty, approx. 2650 B.C. Bird's-eye-view reconstruction. 1. Step pyramid. 2. Mortuary temple of King Zoser. 3. Court containing statue-chamber. 4. Large court with altar. 5. Hall of columns. 6. Court used for Heb-sed (jubilee) festival, with dummy chapels of Upper and Lower Egypt. 7. Small temple. 8. Court in front of Northern Palace. 9. Court of Southern Palace. 10. Empty tomb. 11. Three dummy terraces: in the middle gallery thousands Of vessels were discovered. Cf. p. 68.*

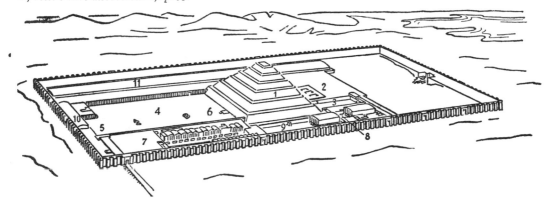

make out the fine curves of the umbel and the triangular cross-section of the stalk.

In front of the step mastaba there is a palace, which — in contrast to the other buildings — was actually accessible; in front of it stood the statue of the king.

The stone blocks used for this building are remarkably small by comparison with those used later. They resemble the mud-bricks in use hitherto, except that they are in stone. The papyrus-cluster columns, which occur for the first time, are engaged in the ends of the walls or else are three-quarter columns; free-standing columns supporting the ceiling are as yet unknown.

The variety in the architecture of the Zoser monument makes for a certain sense of lightness, whereas the pyramids of the IVth Dynasty are monumental, rigid and austere. In these buildings a new style of architecture was developed which conformed to the historical and religious spirit of the age and gave the sculpture, reliefs and architecture of the Pyramid Period their unmistakable unique character. At the beginning of the IVth Dynasty the myth of the resurrection of Osiris was transferred to the god-king, and was represented dramatically during the ceremonial burial-rite, when the deceased became Osiris. Here the temple area no longer serves simply as a place where the pharaoh may hold court in the world beyond, but is also the setting for a specific ritual act.

*Snefru Pyramid* The Pyramids at Giza had forerunners in the three pyramids of the founder of the IVth Dynasty, the pharaoh Snefru, and it was from them that the principle developed on which this complex is based. It can be seen most clearly in the Chephren Pyramid, since this has been best preserved. The Zoser step pyramid was still rectangular in plan, but the so-called Bent Pyramid at Dahshur, built by Snefru, is square. Its name is derived from the fact that the incline is less steep at the bottom than at the top. A pyramid built by the same pharaoh near Meidum remained incomplete, presumably because it was abandoned in favour of a new complex, the so-called 'Red Pyramid', which measures some 99 metres in height. It is still an open question why Snefru built three pyramids. Investigations into the buildings situated around this pyramid are not yet complete. Generally speaking, they seem to correspond in plan to the three huge pyramids at Giza, which are best known to us from the monument to Chephren.

*Chephren Pyramid* The valley temple of the pyramid complex of King Chephren is situated on the edge of the fertile land. It could be reached through two

FIG. 10

gates. In the adjoining hall, which is sited at an oblique angle, embalming was carried out. In the broad pillared hall behind it the sarcophagus was placed, surrounded by statues representing the king: it was here that the ritual of becoming Osiris and the ceremony of 'opening of the mouth' was performed. Afterwards the funerary train proceeded up a covered causeway to the mortuary temple, situated below the pyramid. The front part of this was laid out on the same pattern as in the valley temple. Behind this there was an open court containing 12 shrines with royal statues. In five adjoining chapels there stood five idols. In the mortuary temple the death rites for the pharaoh were carried out. Behind an enclosure wall is the actual tomb, the pyramid with the sarcophagus-chamber inside.

The whole complex of buildings, constructed for ritual purposes, is

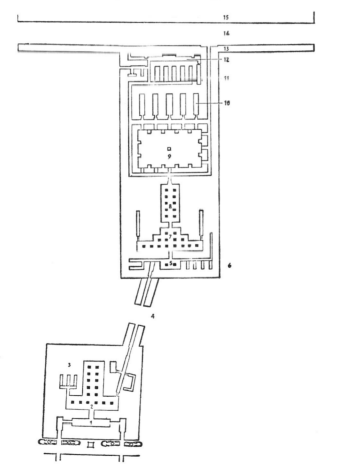

FIG. 10 — *Mortuary temple of King Chephren at Giza. IVth Dynasty, approx. 2500 B.C. Cf. p. 70. Ground-plan.*
*Valley Temple:*
  *1. Ante-room*
  *2. Pillared hall*
  *3. Magazines*
  *4. Causeway*
*Mortuary Temple:*
  *5. Ante-room*
  *6. Magazines*
  *7. Broad hall*
  *8. Long hall*
  *9. Court with statues*
  *10. Statue-chambers*
  *11. Magazines*
  *12. Holy of Holies*
  *13. Internal enclosure wall of pyramid*
  *14. Pyramid court*
  *15. Pyramid*

a magnificent work of architecture. It is one of the gems of ancient Egyptian art.

The individual parts are treated with absolute accuracy from a mathematical and geometrical point of view. The gleaming white pyramid soars up into the blue sky, its lines quite straight despite the fact that the outer facing consists of gigantic blocks, each weighing about 50 cwt. There is barely a millimetre of space between them. The pillars in the temple halls are cut from gigantic monoliths of red granite from Aswan. They are set off against the shimmering alabaster floor, which is light in colour. Inscriptions and reliefs are dispensed with inside the actual temple complex. Only in the processional gallery behind the shrines with the statues in the mortuary temple do we find some reliefs, in limestone, above the granite plinth.

PLATE P. 21    Next to the causeway leading to the Chephren Pyramid lies the Sphinx. It is some 57 metres long and is fashioned out of a knoll of rock. It has the body of a lion and the head of a human being, framed by the royal head-dress. In the course of the thousands of years during which it has stood here, guarding the burial-places of the great pharaohs, it has been buffeted by innumerable sandstorms, and its face shows signs of weathering. The Great Sphinx defies measurement in human terms. It is an image of the god-king, which cannot help but fascinate anyone who looks at it. It is easy to understand why the Greeks took it as symbolic of everything mysterious and enigmatic. No praise can be too high for the technical mastery involved in bringing these colossal masses of stone to the site, and for the magnificent way in which they are handled. Some of the material required was transported down the river from Aswan, some 800 km. away, and then manhandled along a stone ramp — which was either a natural feature or was built especially for the purpose.

*Royal tombs of Vth Dynasty*    Architecture received a different kind of stimulus as a result of the radical change that occurred in intellectual and spiritual life during the Vth Dynasty, which led to a weakening of the role of the god-king and greater emphasis on the finite world. This phenomenon was associated with the cult of the sun-god Rē. The tombs of the sun-kings are far smaller. But from the architectural details it can be seen that they were modelled on naturalistic forms. The temple of King Sahura at Abu Sir, not far from Giza, consists of a valley-gate, causeway, and mortuary temple. The latter has a fine court with palm-frond columns, niches for statues, treasuries and magazines.

Instead of the austere and abstract architecture of the pillars in the

Chephren Temple, that of Sahura contains columns of red granite in imitation of palms, bearing inscriptions in blue. The floor was made of black basalt. The walls had a basalt dado and were decorated above this with painted limestone reliefs. Among the columns suggesting plants, those in the court of the mortuary temple are palmiform, but elsewhere they take the form of clusters of lotus- or papyrus-stalks. Taken in conjunction with the paintings on the walls, they give an impression of life in this earthly world and radiate a sense of gaiety and zest that is carried over into the world of the dead.

FIG. 11

The pyramids built for the first kings of the Vth Dynasty were erected between Giza, Sakkara and Abu Sir, but towards the end of the Vth and in the VIth Dynasty the kings returned once more to Sakkara and built their temples near the Zoser Pyramid.

In the pyramid erected for Unas, last king of the Vth Dynasty, the sarcophagus-chamber inside has, leading off it, a chamber with statue-niches and an offering-chapel, the walls of which are covered with texts recited by the priests during the burial rite. According to Egyptian religious belief these texts freed the deceased from the necessity of going through a systematic burial rite with priests and their own descendants taking part. The insecurity that prevailed at the close

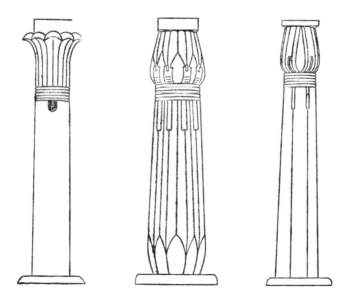

Fig. 11 — Palmiform, papyrus-bundle and lotiform columns. From the mortuary temple of King Sahura at Abu Sir. Vth Dynasty, approx. 2450 B.C. Cf. above

of the Old Kingdom period may have been responsible for this practice of giving the deceased a supply of necessities which would remain unaffected by contemporary developments.

*Sun temples*

FIG. 12

The sun temples which the kings of the Vth Dynasty erected near their pyramids follow the tripartite layout of the temple complexes: a valley temple on the edge of the fertile strip of land and a causeway leading through a gate to an open court, where there stands an obelisk on a plinth. The Egyptians believed that the sun's rays striking its gilded summit transmitted the life-giving force of the sun. In front of the obelisk there stood a huge altar of alabaster. Outside the temple wall of the Sun Temple of Niuserra there was a huge boat, made of brick. This was a model of the celestial barque used by the sun-god Rē. Not much else has survived of the city, palace and temple complexes dating from Old Kingdom times, which were presumably built of non-durable material.

*Private temples*

The temples of courtiers and private persons that were erected at the beginning of the IIIrd Dynasty followed the forms that had developed in the Archaic Period. In the Lower Egyptian burial-places the external wall that faced east had ritual niches to contain offerings for the dead.

Into the rear wall of the niche a limestone plaque was inset depicting

FIG. 12 — *Sun Temple of King Niuserra at Abu Gorab. Reconstruction of the complex, showing the valley temple, causeway, gate and temple court, the latter containing an obelisk and an altar. Vth Dynasty, approx. 2350 B.C. Cf. above*

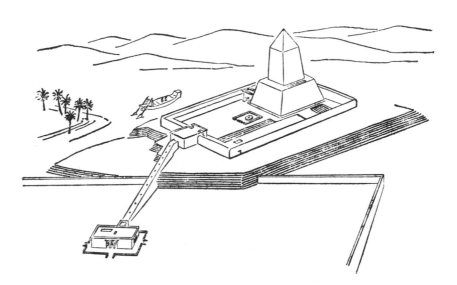

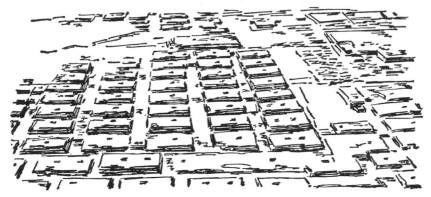

FIG. 13 — *Necropolis of court officials of the IVth Dynasty, situated to the west of the Cheops Pyramid at Giza. Approx. 2590-2470 B.C. Each tomb has a stone superstructure, rectangular in plan, with sloping walls — the so-called mastaba (Arabic: 'bench'). From the top a shaft leads into the subterranean sarcophagus-chamber. The tombs are situated along roads that intersect at right angles. The symmetrical layout of the cemetery probably follows instructions given by King Cheops. Cf. below*

the deceased in front of an offering-table. These are referred to for short as 'dining-table scenes'. The brick tombs of royal princes of the early IVth Dynasty at Meidum contain, in lieu of a niche, a chamber which served as the offering-place. At its western end is a recess like a door, over which appears the all-important representation of the deceased before the offering-table, whereby he was assured of material sustenance in the world beyond. This recess — false door — is the actual place where offerings were made. On the door-post the deceased is depicted in a striding posture, conveying the idea that the lord of the tomb would stride through the door to receive the offerings when he was called to do so by the priest. Behind this chamber is the statue-chamber *(serdab)*, in which stands the *ka* statue of the deceased.

During the course of the IVth Dynasty stone finally came to be used as the building material.

Further development in the form of private tombs was impeded by the fact that standard building regulations were laid down, apparently by the pharaoh Cheops, with regard to the extensive cemetery situated around the pyramids at Giza.

These tombs in the form of mastabas — rectangular tumuli with retaining walls, to which access is gained from the top — are to be found arranged along roads that cross one another at right angles. Instead of the offering-room there is a limestone plaque bearing the 'dining-table scene', let into the outer face of the eastern wall. From

*Tombs at Meidum*

PLATE P. 22

*Giza*

FIG. 13

75

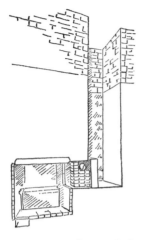

FIG. 14 — *Longitudinal section of a mastaba at Giza. IVth Dynasty, approx. 2590-2470 B.C. The shaft of the tomb has a niche for the 'reserve head' (a substitute for the statue of the deceased usually erected in the statue-chamber). The sarcophagus-chamber is behind. Cf. below*

the top a vertical shaft led into the burial-chamber, which was faced with slabs of white limestone. There was no place for a statue-chamber. Instead of a funerary statue a so-called 'reserve' head was erected in a niche in the shaft. The necropolis ceased to have a uniform character once the royal regulations were no longer applied. Towards the close of the IVth Dynasty the offering-room and *serdab* were again transferred to the interior of the mastaba, and before long a great variety of buildings developed, both at Giza and in the vast necropolis at Sakkara.

*Sakkara*  The tombs of nobles who served as officials, and who became powerful and wealthy during the Vth Dynasty, developed into veritable sepulchral palaces, with a large number of courts and rooms. These are no longer confined to rooms connected with the ritual: offering-room, statue-chamber and sarcophagus-chamber. They became complex, reviving the idea of burial in houses: the tomb of the deceased resembles his dwelling in this world. In the famous tombs of Ti and Ptah-hotep, from the Vth Dynasty, the core of the mastaba, which was originally of massive bulk, is completely broken up. Most of the huge sepulchral palaces now also provide room for the burial of the deceas-  *FIG. 15*  ed's family. The tomb of Mereruka, from the VIth Dynasty, which is the most lavish complex known to us, had 32 rooms. They served to accommodate Mereruka himself, his wife and his son.

To support the architrave square pillars are used. The columns representing plants in the royal mortuary temples were not copied here. With the VIth Dynasty an interesting change comes over sepulchral architecture. The main significance now attaches to the sarcophagus-chamber, which is decorated with carvings in relief representing funerary gifts, and is connected by a door with the statue-chamber. The offering-room disappears completely. Perhaps the uncertain conditions of the times led to doubts as to the desirability of a regular cult of the dead. A sceptical attitude of this kind, which will no doubt have had some justification, may have led to the idea that it would be more effective to give the deceased pictorial representations of offerings on the walls rather than to expose them to the uncertainty and confusion of the age, when there was a rapid turnover among office-holders. It must be borne in mind that according to Egyptian religious beliefs representation also served as a magic invocation, which was deemed to be effective in practice. But the sceptical attitude of the time may also have affected the practical usefulness of the funerary offerings themselves. Great importance could hardly have been attached to them if people were convinced that it was good deeds, not riches and power, that determined the nature of one's existence in the world beyond. Belief in the necessity of funerary rites performed by priests will also have suffered as a consequence of the idea that, since one could not know what the world beyond held in store, one should make the best of this finite world.

Thus the gradual disappearance of vast burial-places has its cause in the material conditions of the age and the spiritual climate that prevailed towards the end of the Old Kingdom. On the other hand the nobility, who had in the meantime attained great power and wealth, now began to erect burial-places in their nomes, far from the capital. During the golden age of the Old Kingdom Upper Egyptian tombs do not play an important part. The necropolises at Qaw el-Kebir and Naga-ed-Deir are unpretentious. In the VIth

*Nomarchs' tombs*

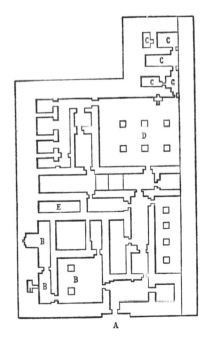

FIG. 15 — *Ground-plan of mastaba of Mereruka at Sakkara. VIth Dynasty, approx. 2320-2160 B.C. Cf. p. 76*
*A — Entrance*
*B — Tomb of Mereruka's wife*
*C — Tomb of Mereruka's son*
*D — Pillared hall*

FIG. 16 — *Limestone relief from Zoser temple complex at Sakkara, showing King Zoser performing a ritual dance. He is wearing the Crown of Upper Egypt and carrying the ceremonial whisk. His ritual race formed part of the festivities connected with the jubilee of his accession to the throne. Above, right: Horus falcon bearing the symbol of life in its talons. Cf. p. 79.*

Dynasty necropolis near Dendera brick is still used for the mastaba. In Upper Egypt, where the river valley is narrow, it was not feasible to build a cemetery such as that at Giza or Sakkara. Thus tombs were cut into the rocky mountain side along both banks of the valley. The rock-cut chamber served as an offering-room, and from this a shaft led into a small burial-chamber. When the nomarch came to inspect his burial site, and admired the delightful view that opened up before him as he looked down from the entrance into the valley, with the green fertile strip of land, the broad river Nile, and the yellow desert, he may well have been filled with a feeling of pleasurable pride in his province.

The rock-cut tombs of the nomarchs at Elephantine, in a mountain opposite what is now the town of Aswan, originate from the era of the VIth Dynasty, but some of them are from the Middle Kingdom. The tombs at Meir, El Bersha and Asyut also illustrate the development of the rock-cut tomb from the end of the Old Kingdom to the Middle Kingdom.

RELIEF AND PAINTING

In Egyptian art compositions executed on a flat surface, such as carvings in relief and paintings, are closely linked to architecture, of which they form a subordinate element. The nature of the carvings in the tombs is determined by the dimensions of those parts of the wall where they are placed. They do not continue round corners on to adjoining walls. Instead each wall is treated as a unit, the last figures being turned inwards to face the middle.

Just as architecture provided a setting for ritual and developed in accordance with the changes that took place in religious ideas, so also reliefs and paintings derived their purpose and meaning from magic and religion.

The historical and religious assumptions held by the ancient Egypt-

FIG. 17 — *Relief in wood from the tomb of Hesy-ra at Sakkara. Hesy-ra is shown with sceptre, staff and writing material. IIIrd Dynasty, approx. 2660-2590 B.C. Egyptian Museum, Cairo. Height 1.14 m. Cf. below*

ians became modified over the course of millennia, and these changes were reflected in their funerary art: yet it always remained its function to provide the prerequisites for life in the world beyond, just as the temples served to represent the links between the god-king and the celestial powers.

So far as style is concerned, the reliefs carved during the IIIrd Dynasty continue in the tradition established by the Narmer palette in the early period, although they do not represent historical events as this did.

Several reliefs from the Zoser period portray the king in a striding posture or performing a ritual dance, with taut body and muscles. Here, as in the case of the relief of King Semerkhet carved from the rock in Sinai, the slight awkwardness apparent in the Narmer palette has been overcome. The large amount of narrative detail has been translated into a monumental pictorial representation in which the individual elements are clearly defined, with a tendency towards solidity. The reliefs in private tombs from the IIIrd Dynasty are remarkable for their compactness and clarity of composition. On human figures the tendons of the muscles, collar-bone and joints are elaborately modelled, giving the works a buoyant vitality.

In the reliefs of the Hesy-ra tomb we find two motifs rendered according to a convention that henceforward formed part of the established canon in sepulchral art: the lord of the tomb striding along, in a manner that recurs time and again on false doors, and the 'dining-table scene' already mentioned. The inscription that has been added is not yet divided into separate lines, but the hieroglyphs are arranged so harmoniously that, from the standpoint of meaning as well as of style, they form a balanced entity with the figure, which after all is also a symbolic pictograph.

In tombs of royal princes at Meidum from the beginning of the IVth Dynasty the offering-rooms in the core of the mastaba had walls faced with limestone slabs which afforded ample space for carvings in relief. There are effigies of the lord of the tomb, who is rendered on a disproportionately large scale, receiving funerary gifts from men and women, and also scenes depicting the slaughtering of sacrificial

FIG. 16

FIG. 17

*IVth Dynasty tombs at Meidum*

79

cattle. These reliefs are to be found near the false door, and are designed to supplement the offerings made there by priests and relatives of the deceased, in order to ensure his wants in the after-life. The scenes portraying men tilling the fields, trapping birds, fishing, and hunting game in the desert convey an idea of everyday life in ancient Egypt; they are arranged in narrow horizontal panels. Generally speaking, the figures are not shown at a particular moment of action, but in a posture characteristic of the occupation concerned. The scene thus expresses the concept 'action' itself, rather than a specific task being performed by a certain person at a certain time. The sense of movement has been conventionalized into a schematic posture. A group of persons is depicted by arranging them in a file, or else identical objects are represented in the form of an echelon, with their outlines parallel. To characterize particular categories of persons a scheme is developed whereby it is possible to distinguish between officials, servants and foreigners by their clothing, attributes and posture.

In addition to the majestic clean-cut raised reliefs, another technique was adopted, in the tomb of Nefermaat at Meidum, which was to affect the durability of the carving. The figures were incised very deeply, as in a sunk relief, and the depressions filled in with various kinds of coloured paste. This new technique was, however, soon abandoned, since the coloured paste easily dropped out.

In the tomb of Princess Atet at Meidum the walls are not lined with limestone slabs but coated with plaster, and on this figures were then PLATE P. 23 painted. From this tomb the panel of geese is unfortunately almost the only painting that has survived. It formed a sub-register of a large wall-painting that showed birds being trapped by means of a clap-net. The geese are rendered in a manner that testifies to a keen sense of observation on the part of the artist, to his knowledge of animals, and to a naive delight in naturalistic representation. The range of colours in the reliefs and the paste used to fill in the depressions was very limited, but on the other hand the nuances of shades in the painting produce a sense of spontaneous vitality.

Many and varied were the endeavours made at the beginning of the IVth Dynasty to arrive at some final form for the style and technique of funerary scenes, such as was developed by the succeeding generation of Cheops, utilizing the wealth of opportunities opened up by the IIIrd Dynasty and the age of Snefru.

*Tombs at Giza* When considering the architecture of the tombs we noted how little enthusiasm there was for pictorial representation during the Pyramid Period. Only a few examples have survived that permit us to judge the style of the reliefs in the royal buildings. The private tombs at Giza, too, which contained neither an offering-room nor a statue-chamber, offered no opportunity for continuing the rich tradition begun in the earlier part of the IVth Dynasty. Carving in relief was confined to the 'dining-table scene' let into the outer wall of the tomb. In the tablet from the tomb of Wepemnofret the occupant is depicted wearing a cloak of panther-skin, seated on a stool with legs like those of an ox, before a table on which are some pieces of bread. In front of his head are a wash-basin and water-jug, over which his name appears. The hieroglyphic signs above and below the offering-table denote various gifts. In the right-hand part of the relief a list is given of four different kinds of textiles. The horizontal row of hieroglyphs at the top and the two vertical ones on the right-hand side contain Wepemnofret's titles. The figure and the hieroglyphs are divided by raised vertical and horizontal lines, but together they form a meaningful whole. The well-proportioned division of the plane accords with the clarity and austerity of the Pyramid Period. In portraying the human figure the Egyptian artist proceeds from natural models. But what he conveys is not a portrait as seen through his own eyes, which would necessarily be subjective; instead, basing himself upon his own experience and ideas, he fashions an image that expresses in generalized and schematic terms the nature of 'man' as such. What he is concerned to create is not a likeness but a symbol. The artist represents the figure by broad areas and makes it whole by adding individual parts bounded by outlines. Thus the head is shown in profile, but the eye, shoulders and body are viewed frontally, while the legs once again are rendered in profile. Each single part is given a form that is appropriate to its meaning, and the figure as a whole has a message valid for eternity. The deceased is depicted in a calm contemplative mood, never performing an action. The belief in the magic properties of images produced to last for ever necessitated a scheme of representation that had no place for random features. Egyptian carving in relief is thus unaware of foreshortening, perspective, depth, shadow, or the concept of space; nor is it possible to identify the age or individual characteristics of the deceased. The title and name are the only clues that enable one to ascertain for whom the relief was carved. The most important element used in composition is the line. The outline is drawn in such a way as to form acute

PLATE P. 24

*Style*

angles. The linear style is suited to work on a plane surface. There are no projections and none of the figures is turned to face the observer.

In painting reliefs, too, the artist works from life, but follows a colour scheme that does not correspond to that of his subject. The background is painted grey and blue, while for the figure various colours are used, ranging from red, yellow, white and blue to black and green. The pigment is obtained from mineral substances; unrefracted colours alone occur.

*The artist*  The sculptors and painters who have left us such sumptuous testimony of their skill were artisans. In the Egyptian language, characteristically enough, there is no word for 'art' or 'artist'; a sculptor is denoted by a hieroglyph showing a bow-drill. Prime importance attaches to workmanship rather than to artistic imagination. The function which the sculptor had to perform left him no opportunity to develop an individual style; for he was not expected to express his subjective experience but to reproduce an object of eternal value in accordance with a definite schematic pattern. A community of artisans in a workshop worked out the rules, which were handed down to later generations.

Unfortunately no works have been preserved which provide information about the way in which reliefs and paintings were produced. But some conclusions about this may be drawn from tombs that were left unfinished. The carving of a relief began with the division of the
Fig. 18  plane into units for purposes of measurement. With the aid of these divisions the figures and objects were drawn in. After this the sculptor set to work. First he drew the contour lines with a copper chisel, and then hollowed out the space around the figure.

He did not, of course, always keep strictly to the drawing. The next stage was the modelling of the figure. Finally, the surface was overlaid with a coating of plaster, which was painted by another artist.

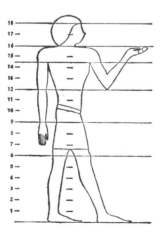

Fig. 18 — *Canon used in the Old Kingdom for making preliminary outline before drawing a human figure. Cf. above · p. 120 .*

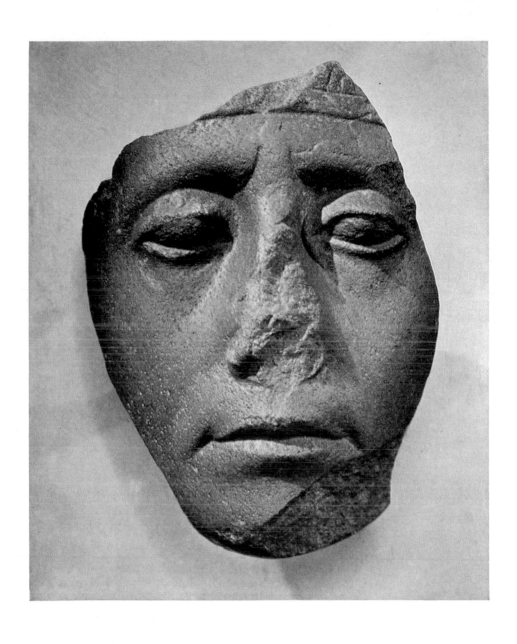

PLATE 19 — Head of Sesostris III. Brown stone. Middle Kingdom, XIIth Dynasty, approx. 1850 B.C. *Metropolitan Museum, New York. Height 16 cm. Cf. p. 127.*

PLATE 20 — Nubian soldiers with bows and arrows. Painted wooden model. From the tomb of the nomarch Mesehti at Asyut. Middle Kingdom, XIth Dynasty, approx. 2000 B.C. *Egyptian Museum, Cairo. Height approx. 40 cm. Cf. p. 130.*

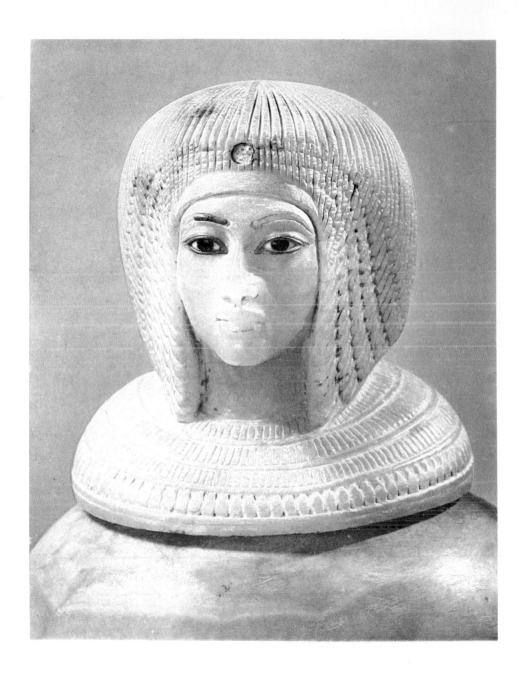

PLATE 21 — Alabaster lid of a canopic jar, in the shape of a queen's head. From a concealed place in the Valley of the Kings near Thebes. New Kingdom, XVIIIth Dynasty, Amarna Period, approx. 1350 B.C. *Egyptian Museum, Cairo. Total height of canopic jar 36 cm. Cf. pp. 148, 207.*

PLATE 22 — Gold pendant in the shape of a fish. From Illahun. Middle Kingdom, approx. 1900 B.C. *Royal Scottish Museum, Edinburgh. Length 3.4 cm. Cf. p. 130.*

PLATE 29 — Statuette of the priestess Imeret-nebes. Painted wood. Middle Kingdom, XIIth Dynasty, 1991-1785 B.C. *Rijksmuseum van Oudheden, Leyden. Height 86 cm. Cf. p. 130.*

PLATE 24 — Temple at Luxor in Thebes. Court of Amenophis II, containing papyrus-bundle columns. New Kingdom, XVIIIth Dynasty, 1400-1362 B.C. *Cf. p. 154.*

PLATE 25 — Mortuary Temple of Queen Hatshepsut at Deir el-Bahari, on the western bank of the river at Thebes. New Kingdom, XVIIIth Dynasty, approx. 1480 B.C. *Cf. p. 156.*

PLATE 26 — Detail of limestone reliefs in the Mortuary Temple of Queen Hatshepsut at Deir el-Bahari, Thebes. XVIIIth Dynasty, 1490—approx. 1470 B.C.

PLATE 27   Detail of a wall-painting showing birds being hunted with a wooden throw-stick. From a tomb at Thebes. New Kingdom, XVIIIth Dynasty, approx. 1400 B.C. *British Museum. Cf. p. 167.*

PLATE 29 — Female musicians: detail of a banqueting scene in the tomb of the priest Nakht at Thebes. New Kingdom, XVIIIth Dynasty, approx. 1425 B.C. *Cf. p. 168.*

PLATE 28 — Detail of a banqueting scene in the tomb of Menna at Thebes, showing Menna's wife. New Kingdom, XVIIIth Dynasty, approx. 1422-1411 B.C. *Cf. p. 168.*

PLATE 30 — Lady-in-waiting: detail of a limestone relief representing a festive gathering, in the tomb of the vizier Ramose at Thebes. New Kingdom, XVIIIth Dynasty, approx. 1400-1362 B.C. *Cf. p. 169.*

Thus many hands were invariably involved in the creation of a single work, and each person was responsible only for part of the process. Adherence to a strict canon impeded the development of artistic individuality, but on the other hand this has been true of sculpture in all ages, and has had the function of keeping up standards.

Just as Egyptian art was not the work of creative artists in our sense of the term, so also it dispensed with the person of the viewer. Reliefs and statues in tombs were not visible to the passer-by. When the deceased was interred the shaft leading into the tomb was blocked with slabs of stone. The works were not made to be admired from an aesthetic point of view: they fulfilled a ritual function by their very existence.

The schematization which evolved in reliefs and painting during the Pyramid Period corresponds in style and spirit to the Egyptian genius. It illustrates in a clear and most emphatic manner the inclination of the Egyptian artist to strict linear treatment, his tendency towards formalism, as a result of which he turns real phenomena into symbols. During the centuries that followed these characteristics developed to a peak of perfection. They also underwent certain modifications, as new elements were added to the canon. The general sense of this evolutionary process was away from symbolism and in the direction of naturalistic representation. But even where the widest differentiations occur, the form and content evolved during the Pyramid Period remain in evidence. In a general sense, they are binding upon the whole of Egyptian art.

Towards the close of the IVth Dynasty, when there was once again a tendency to build spacious offering-rooms in tombs, greater attention came to be given to reliefs. To the subjects that had been treated in the tombs at Meidum new motifs were now added.

The place of ritual, with the 'dining-table scene', becomes a representation of the funerary feast, from which music and dancing are not absent. The funerary furnishings are depicted in detail, reproducing individual phases in their manufacture. Some of the new motifs and the way in which they are treated herald new attitudes of mind, which during the ensuing period were to provide the arts with a different framework.

According to the doctrine of Heliopolis nature is constantly revived *Vth Dynasty* through the sequence of seasons by the sun-god Rē, the preserver of all living things. He is the guarantor of the eternal cosmic order. His actions are related to the visible finite world, which as a consequence is entitled to its place in the perfect divine order. The development of religious ideas along these lines explains why men who desired an after-life should favour pictorial representations of this earthly world: the answer lies in their delight in the divinely-ordained perfection of the world in which they lived. This is the source of the numerous scenes depicting everyday life which are to be found in Vth Dynasty temples and tombs.

The world beyond is thought to be in the east, in the 'Field of Rushes', where the sun rises each morning. It is thither that the deceased journeys in his barque, passing through a land abounding in fauna and *Reliefs on royal* flora. The painted walls of the royal monuments depict, in a very *monuments* shallow relief distinguished by delicate modelling, the king performing ritual acts or keeping company with the gods.

In reliefs from the tomb of Sahura the ancient theme of triumph over vanquished enemies is taken up again: four gods can be seen bringing to the king captives bound by ropes. From their features it FIG. 19 is clear that they are Africans, Libyans and Asiatics.

Another relief shows the booty taken during a campaign against the Libyans, and may well refer to a particular historical event.

Hunting scenes have lost some of their rigidity. The desert is represented as undulating terrain, where a wide variety of plants grow. The diverse individual motifs, which are newly formulated, retain their intrinsic value in the composition as a whole. The reliefs depicting the seasons in the temple of King Niuserra show the delight taken in portraying flora and fauna. These reliefs may be regarded as an exposition of the doctrine of Heliopolis. The various operations involved in tilling the fields and bringing in the harvest are arranged in meaningful fashion. They depict the life of a fellah in the course of a single year. 13

During the troubled times of the VIth Dynasty such spirited pictures of everyday life were banned from the temples.

*Sakkara* The colossal sepulchral palaces of the court officials of the Vth Dynasty offered an ideal opportunity for relief work on a grand scale. It is here that we find the greatest number of cult scenes, as well as subjects taken from everyday life, in which the artist was allowed to FIG. 20 give his imagination free rein. The famous tombs of Ti and Ptahhotep at Sakkara, and also the tombs dating from the first half of the VIth Dynasty, give an impressive picture of the sweeping changes that took place in the Egyptian world-outlook during this era. In spite of its dynamism the bubbling vitality is subjected to linear treatment

FIG. 20 — *Fording a river with a herd of cattle. Detail from a limestone relief in the tomb of Ti at Sakkara. Vth Dynasty, approx. 2470-2320 B.C. Cf. p. 96.*

of the plane. The rendering of objects is still standardized. The posture of the figures and the manner of depicting group compositions follows a new scheme, which seeks the general in the particular. The action presented is not related to a definite place or time, but is still 'action as such', a pure concept free from random attributes. The figure of the lord of the tomb remains unaffected by the dynamism in the numerous panels, which are arranged one above the other. He is, so to speak, the silent observer of the scenes about him. He is shown with his left leg before the right, as though striding forward; in his outstretched left hand he is holding a long staff, while the right

FIG. 19 — *Captives in bonds. Limestone relief from the mortuary temple of King Sahura at Abu Sir. Detail of a scene showing four gods leading the prisoners to the king. Vth Dynasty, approx. 2400 B.C. Berlin. Cf. p.96.*

arm hangs down. The most important figure, the man for whom all this pictorial wealth has been produced, stands out on account of his disproportionately large size.

In IVth Dynasty reliefs the individual figures were arranged one after the other, without overlapping. Where a group of people was to be depicted, several figures were placed in echelon behind one another, in such a manner that their outlines ran parallel. This resulted in a kind of enumeration, but there was no evident relationship between the individual figures. This system could not suffice to portray men in action, and it is therefore not surprising that it should have become more flexible during the course of the Vth Dynasty. The individual figures are now combined to form a group, in that they turn to face one another in the performance of some common task. The body itself is no longer shown in a static posture. Often one shoulder is turned towards the front; foreshortening and overlapping are not ruled out so strictly as before. Occasionally a figure is portrayed with the head turned backwards, in order to indicate a relationship to the person behind him; the effect is enhanced by lively gestures. The inscriptions on the reliefs often elucidate their content in a humorous fashion. Sometimes they consist of a speech and a rejoinder.

*Reliefs from the VIth Dynasty* In the course of the VIth Dynasty further innovations come to be made. Reliefs now depict earthly existence in all its manifold abundance — so much so that their original purpose, to serve the deceased, recedes ever further into the background.

The disintegration of the state order at the close of the Old Kingdom raised doubts in the Egyptians' minds about the joyous attitude to life adopted by their fathers. In their mood of scepticism they began to wonder whether all the ostentatious splendour in tombs was really of use to the dead. Another consideration was that during these troubled times it did not seem desirable to interpret the world beyond as a replica of this world. The result was a greater emphasis on cult scenes. In the unpretentious tombs of court officials at the close of the VIth Dynasty the funerary offerings are represented in the sarcophagus-chamber, and the offering-room loses its former importance. In lieu of carvings showing life on earth, servant figurines and models of granaries, byres, etc. were placed in the tombs.

SCULPTURE IN THE ROUND Sculpture in the round, like architecture, painting and reliefs, served the ancient Egyptians as a means of representing their religious ideas. Royal statues in the mortuary temple and statues in private tombs have a particular function to fulfil in the death rite. Egyptians believed that the statues of private persons which were erected in the statue-chambers inside the tombs were imbued with the *ka*, the immortal soul, of the deceased. They symbolized the fact that the occupant of the tomb would live for evermore. This required that he should be represented in an idealized manner, without any individual touches being added.

Egyptian sculpture of the Old Kingdom period is extremely compact and is conceived two-dimensionally, in the manner of a drawing. It is contained within the right-angled planes of the cube or pillar. Modelled human figures are static and orientated solely towards a profile or a frontal view. This manner of treatment makes it impossible, for example, for an arm to be stretched out diagonally, or for the head to be turned sideways. The proportions are modelled on those found in real life, and are based on a fixed system. Before the block is worked the horizontal and vertical axes are marked out with paint. The basic unit of measurement is the human fist, which is one-eighteenth of the total height of the figure. The work that results from the application of this scheme is a truly artistic expression of the concept 'man'. It has a timeless quality. Only when a title and name have been added can the figure be related to a particular person — the individual who is here immortalized for ever.

All sculpture in the Old Kingdom was painted, regardless of the fact whether the material was limestone or coloured hard stone; only the red granite from Aswan is an occasional exception to the rule. Men's bodies were painted reddish-brown, women's light yellow. The seat and plinth are painted white or black. White garments are sometimes outlined in red. The wig, eyebrows and beard are black; eyes are suggested by means of various kinds of material. As was the case on relief works, the painting on sculptured figures was not executed in a naturalistic style.

Sculpture in the round, like paintings and reliefs, underwent variations during the Old Kingdom in accordance with changes of style. A life-size statue of King Zoser, the founder of the IIIrd Dynasty, is the first illustration in monumental form of the god-king's pretensions to absolute power. There is a strict cubism in the block-shaped forms of which it is built up — although this is somewhat marred by the awkward posture of the arms. The pronounced cheek-bones and full lips give the face a look of sombre imperiousness. With this statue a convention has been established for the representation of human beings in monumental sculpture in the round — although it still

*IIIrd Dynasty*

FIG. 21

lacks a sense of freedom and equipoise, and the process of stylistic development is not yet complete. In sculptured figures of private persons from the IIIrd Dynasty we can see even more distinctly the quest for finality in the means of expression. The funerary statues, most of which are less than life-size, are thick-set and give an impression of clumsiness. At the beginning of the Old Kingdom the most prominent part was played by seated figures, with granite as the favourite material.

*IVth Dynasty* To represent IVth Dynasty statuary we have a diorite figure of King Chephren which expresses well the genius of the Pyramid Period. PLATE P. 25 It is one of 23 statues erected in the valley temple of the royal tombs at Giza. They were used by the priests during the burial ceremonies when performing the rite of becoming Osiris, which made the god-king of this world one of the great gods of the world beyond.

The king is seated upon a cube-shaped throne, which in front merges into a foot-support and at the back has a pillar reaching up as far as the shoulders. Its legs are suggested by lions worked in relief. On the sides is the hieroglyph denoting the 'union of the Two Lands', carved in high relief. On the foot-support the king's title and name are engraved. The posture of the seated pharaoh conveys a sense of austere static majesty. His right hand is clenched, with the thumb upwards, and rests upon the thigh, the left hand is stretched out flat on the left knee. The legs are placed side by side. The limbs are not yet detached from the body — the arms are close to the body, while the legs are connected to the edge of the seat by a fillet of stone. The sculpture is completely subordinated to the planes of the block, which are accentuated most heavily in the foot-support and at the back; nowhere are they broken by projections. The face is framed by the royal head-dress, featuring

FIG. 21 — *Limestone statue of King Zoser from the Zoser temple complex at Sakkara. IIIrd Dynasty, approx. 2660-2590 B.C. Egyptian Museum, Cairo. Slightly less than life-size. Cf. p. 99.*

the uraeus snake — an attribute of gods and kings — carved in low relief. Below the chin is the royal beard which, like the headgear, forms part of the pharaonic ceremonial costume. Round the loins is a short linen kilt. Perched on the back-pillar is the Horus falcon, whose divine nature is manifest in the person of the pharaoh. Its wings are outspread, encompassing Chephren's head. The body is exquisitely modelled down to the last detail. From it, as from the powerful face, there radiates a tense vitality.

There is nothing unique or individual in such images as these. The god-king embodies the universal: an eternal existence that triumphs over mere temporal fate. He appears before us as the expression of a cosmic order in which man has been raised up beyond the limits of the phenomenal world, with all its confusion and chaos, by his pretensions to divinity, and has attained eternal life among the gods. But soon, however, this matchless combination of two worlds is left behind: the artistic genius moves on, and already in the statues of Mycerinus, Chephren's successor on the throne of the pharaohs, a gradual change in form and manner of expression may be noted. Scenic compositions now appear in which Mycerinus is depicted striding along beside his consort, or between various gods. 14 His queen is shown with her arm around him and her hand resting upon his arm or body. This posture creates the impression that she is slightly less prominent than the pharaoh himself. The fact that the latter should be depicted in conjunction with his consort indicates a closer approximation to the terrestrial world. It may be regarded as implying a gradual diminution of the king's claim to be divine. In the ensuing period royal images to an increasing extent come to have a realistic character. The tendency is towards portraiture.

Only a few figures of commoners have survived from the IVth Dynasty. They continue the strict geometrical structure and squat form found with figures in the round dating from the IIIrd Dynasty. An exception is the group of statues of Prince Rahotep, one of the sons of King Snefru and his spouse Nofret. They were found in the statue-chamber of their tomb at Meidum, near the pyramid of King Snefru. The royal couple are seated upon a cube-shaped stool, which at the back has a support almost as tall as the figures themselves. It bears an engraved inscription giving their names and titles. Rahotep, clad in a short white kilt, is depicted with his right hand clenched against his chest, while his left hand, with the thumb pointing upwards, rests on the upper part of his thigh. The torso is powerful, with broad

PLATES PP. 26, 43

shoulders; the facial features express sturdiness, energy and intelligence, and this effect is enhanced by the inlaid eyes. Princess Nofret, on the other hand, seems tender and pensive. Her femininity is suggested beneath her long white robe. On her forehead, below the artificial wig, one can see her natural hair. The headband with painted flowers and the gay collar necklace form a colourful contrast to the yellow tint of her skin and the white of the garment and the back-pillar of the throne.

These two statues were erected side by side in the tomb, producing the effect of a sculptured group. The two figures are enclosed by the plinth and especially by the high supporting pillar. This is a characteristic way of illustrating the concept of a compact cubic space, into which the sculpture is placed.

FIG. 22    The tombs in the necropolis at Giza, as has already been pointed out, had insufficient space for the erection of funerary statues. Instead so-called 'reserve heads' were placed in a niche in the wall of the shaft leading to the sarcophagus-chamber. Among these heads there are some very impressive images which seem to represent the personal qualities of the person portrayed. The fact that no space was available for an inscription giving the name of the lord of the tomb may perhaps have led to the rendering of distinguishable facial features. As soon as room became available in the tomb for the erection of a funerary statue, 'reserve heads' ceased to be made, since they were no more than a makeshift device.

PLATE P. 46    The limestone bust of Prince Ankh-haf is unusual. It was found in a brick building added to a stone mastaba at Giza. It was presumably erected on a low base built against the wall. The shape of this bust is almost unique in Egypt. In this case, as in that of the 'reserve heads', we have no more than a makeshift device. The surface of the stone is coated with a layer of plaster, such as is also to be found in reliefs produced at this time. This helped the sculptor to carve the figure,

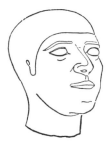

FIG. 22 — 'Reserve head' from a mastaba in the IVth Dynasty necropolis at Giza. Approx. 2590-2470 B.C. In IVth Dynasty tombs there was no room for a statue-chamber in which to erect a funerary statue, and therefore a so-called 'reserve head' was placed in a niche in the shaft of the tomb. Egyptian Museum, Cairo. Height 19.5 cm. Cf. above

since plaster can be worked effortlessly, and lends itself more readily than hard and brittle stone to realistic treatment of fine details.

The sculptured bust of Ankh-haf has a vitality and expressiveness hitherto unknown. Skilled craftsmanship and a keen sense of observation have here resulted in an outstanding likeness. The line of the eyebrows, the indication of the folds of the eyelids and lachrymal bags, the lines between the nostrils and the corners of the mouth — all these features make it apparent that Ankh-haf was a personage of distinction. In contrast to the 'reserve heads', which are left unpainted, this bust is painted reddish-brown.

While making these superb attempts at naturalistic treatment, Egyptian sculptors also continue to represent men as timeless and impersonal.

The establishment of an orderly administration during the IIIrd Dynasty made the profession of scribe one of the most important court offices. A particular convention was developed in order to represent such persons. They were shown in a squatting posture, with legs crossed. The Vth Dynasty is the heyday of the court bureaucracy, when officials of noble origin gradually achieved an independent status. Thus it is not surprising that at this time statuettes representing scribes should have attained their final form. The famous limestone statue of Kay, a judge and nomarch, has a plainly discernible vitality about it. It was found in his tomb at Sakkara and is now in the Louvre. Kay is depicted squatting on the ground, with legs crossed; the arms are detached from the body, and the neck rises up boldly from the shoulders. With his left hand he is holding a papyrus scroll and his right hand, modelled in such a way as to bring out the finest details, once held a reed (a writing implement). The austere face with the skilfully inlaid eyes gives an impression of shrewdness and alertness. Several statues of scribes have been found which are replicas of this one. Despite all the individual characteristics features, it remains symbolic of the class of professional scribes as such, and thus a standard which other works of this kind were obliged to copy.

The variety of subjects and the dynamic style of two-dimensional art during the Vth Dynasty have their corollary in sculpture, where we find a rich choice of styles and an imaginative treatment of detail, with a tendency towards naturalism. Thus statue groups, which are first introduced under Mycerinus during the IVth Dynasty, also occur in the case of commoners during the Vth Dynasty.

*Vth Dynasty*

PLATE P. 44

When less importance came to be attached to offering-rooms, servant figurines were produced to afford the deceased protection in the world beyond. These statuettes, found in the sarcophagus-chambers of tombs, gradually superseded the cycles of reliefs, which were no longer produced. Among these servant figurines are brewers of beer, PLATE P. 45 slaughterers, bakers, and even potters. They have unusual vitality, since the subjects are shown performing their daily tasks. Their importance lies less in their artistic quality than in the information yielded by this kind of theme. Towards the close of the Old Kingdom these servant figurines are superseded by models carved in wood *Wooden carvings* which, in the manner of a doll's house, show events in a slaughter-house, in a weaving-mill, or at a cattle-market.

Fresh opportunities are also opened up before sculptors in wood during the Vth Dynasty. This material can be carved easily, and thus permits fine elaborate workmanship. In most cases the limbs (especially the arms) are made separately and are affixed by means of pegs. In some of the best works, such as the 'Village Magistrate', 15 sculpture in wood reaches a peak of perfection. On the other hand, there is no artistic value in the mass-produced wooden servant figurines. Little has survived in the way of handicrafts, since in the Pyramid Period lists of offerings and reliefs took the place of funerary gifts. There are alabaster jars for storing ointment and various kinds of oil. Particularly impressive is the superb jewellery that was made, PLATE P. 63 exemplified by the gold collar necklace found in the tomb of Impy. *VIth Dynasty* From the VIth Dynasty only one royal figure has survived. It was erected in the temple at Hierakonpolis in Upper Egypt, and is a copper statue of Pepi I and his young son Merenra. 16 The features of the king no longer suggest divine majesty, but rather the traits of a man grown mature with experience. The boy, on the other hand, has a worldly cheerful expression. With their polished copper surface, inlaid eyes and gilded details these statues must have appeared particularly valuable. They could, however, scarcely convey the animated naturalism of a painted stone or wooden statue.

Thus this group, the first to be erected in a temple dedicated to the gods, seems to have been set up with the object of impressing those who beheld it. This heralded a new aim on the part of carvers of royal portraits, which was to find consummation in the temple statues of the Middle Kingdom.

As its spiritual content waned, funerary sculpture lost its artistic form, and figures came to be treated roughly and summarily.

# VII. THE MIDDLE KINGDOM

In approx. 2040 B.C. the Theban family of nomarchs succeeded in putting an end to the internecine strife that had brought about the collapse of the Old Kingdom. After the fall of a family of Herakleopolitan nomarchs, who ruled over Lower Egypt, Mentuhotep II was able to unite the entire country under his dominion. In the list of pharaohs his reign is given as the first in the XIth Dynasty, and thus the first in the history of the Middle Kingdom. *HISTORICAL SURVEY*

The re-unification of Egypt by Mentuhotep II — the opening of a new era, the Middle Kingdom — took place under conditions very different from those that had pertained when the country became united for the first time, under Menes in the early dynastic period. By the end of the Old Kingdom the nomarchs of the individual nomes had become powerful independent rulers. The new king, who sprang from their ranks, succeeded in winning recognition by the other nomes, but could hardly claim the veneration due to a god. Recollections of the time of troubles were still alive among the people. The god-kings had proved wanting, and for this reason the significance of the monarchy underwent a sweeping transformation. It was not until the XIIth Dynasty that it again acquired absolute power, based upon the allegiance of a new court aristocracy and a middle class that now enjoyed a certain prestige. Nomarchs and priests play a very minor role during this period. *Mentuhotep II*

The kings of the XIth Dynasty seem to have ruled without engaging in warfare against domestic enemies. During the reign of Mentuhotep III an expedition was despatched to the quarries at Wadi Hammamat and to Punt, the land of fragrant incense. It is said that the last seven years of the dynasty were a time of internecine strife between members of the ruling house. Mentuhotep IV, the last king of this line, was apparently deposed by his vizier Amenemhat, who claimed the throne and founded the XIIth Dynasty. The next 206 years were an era of power and glory. In order to safeguard continuity of succession, Amenemhat I, after ruling over the country for twenty years, appointed his son, Sesostris, to share the throne as co-regent. The main task that faced the rulers of the XIIth Dynasty was to maintain order at home. *XIth Dynasty* *XIIth Dynasty*

The subjugation of Nubia was begun by Sesostris I and brought to completion by Sesostris III. A stele erected near the fortress at Semna, MAP P. 235

by the Second Cataract, records the fact that Semna was the southern boundary of Egypt. Control over the Nile valley in Nubia was assured by the construction of fortresses. Strategic points were also set up along the route from Coptos in Upper Egypt to the Red Sea, which gave access to Sinai and Punt, the land of incense, on the Somali coast. From archaeological finds it may be inferred that trade was carried on with Crete and Asia Minor.

The campaigns of Sesostris III not only consolidated Egypt's control of Nubia as far as the Second Cataract, but also led to the conquest of southern Palestine. These successes ensured the security of Egypt's borders and gave her a position of undisputed hegemony in the Near East.

Amenemhat III, who succeeded Sesostris III, was able to devote himself exclusively to domestic problems. His predecessors on the throne had already begun to reclaim the Faiyum for agricultural purposes, and it became the most fertile part of the country. It was irrigated by a network of canals, dams and sluices that ran between one of the arms of the Nile (nowadays known as Bahr Yusuf) and Lake Moeris. On the edge of this oasis, near Hawara, the pharaoh built his tomb, which *XIIIth-XIVth* was well known in antiquity as 'the Labyrinth'. The line of kings *Dynasties* that includes the names of Amenemhat and Sesostris comes to a close with Amenemhat IV, who appears almost invariably as co-regent with his father. He was succeeded by a number of kings bearing the name of Sebekhotep, who are reckoned as the XIIIth Dynasty. Their rule lasted for some 55 years, and followed upon an initial period of convulsion, the effects of which were never completely overcome. The numerous names of pharaohs of the XIVth Dynasty listed in the royal papyrus at Turin refer to illegitimate petty princes who never ruled over the entire country.

From the end of the XIIth Dynasty onwards the progressive disintegration of the country so weakened it that hardly any resistance could be offered to foreign invaders in the Delta. The conquest of Egypt by the Hyksos put an end to the Middle Kingdom.

*'Hyksos';* The term 'Hyksos' is not a proper name but means 'foreign rulers'. *XVth-XVIth* The Hyksos were presumably a group of peoples driven from Asia *Dynasties* Minor by the advancing Hurri, who immigrated into the region of the Euphrates from the Armenian highlands. The Hyksos conquered Egypt and ruled it as the XVth Dynasty.

The XVIth Dynasty comprised another group of Hyksos rulers whose dominion extended only over Lower Egypt.

During this period a struggle for emancipation from foreign rule could be initiated in the independent southern part of the country. This movement was led by Theban nomarchs who are reckoned as the XVIIth Dynasty.

During the turbulent Hyksos era, known as the 'Second Intermediate Period', cultural life came to an almost complete standstill.

Religious beliefs had already undergone a process of radical transformation during the closing phase of the Old Kingdom. The collapse of the state order and the reaction against sacrosanct monarchy encouraged the people to put their faith in magic and superstition. On the other hand, the sceptical outlook common among the privileged classes led to the growth of a spiritual ethic according to which men's moral conduct was the criterion that determined whether they were to enjoy happiness in the after-life.

Already in the Old Kingdom there is evidence of the idea of a 'last judgment', presided over by the sun-god Rē. In the Middle Kingdom this concept is related to the Osiris myth. In the Old Kingdom divine judges are invoked to regulate legal relationships between men, but in the Middle Kingdom they pass judgment on the relationship between men and god, on their morals. The recognition of vices and failings lead to the view that man is responsible to God for his own conduct.

As the instructions for King Merikere put it:

> 'The judges who judge the oppressed,
> thou knowest that they are not lenient on that day of judging the miserable,
> in the hour of carrying out the decision.
> Ill fareth it when the accuser is the Wise One [Thoth, god of wisdom].
> Put not thy trust in length of years;
> they [the judges of the dead] regard the lifetime as an hour.
> A man remaineth over after death and his deeds are placed beside him in heaps.
>
> But it is for eternity that one is there
> [in the other world], and he is a fool
> that maketh light of the judges of the dead.
> But he that cometh unto them without wrong-doing,
> he shall continue yonder like a god,
> stepping boldly forward like the Lords of Eternity.' 17

At a later stage the plea to the judges of the nether world generally takes the form of a 'negative confession': that is to say, the deceased enumerates various failings and sins, emphasizing the fact that he has not committed them.

PLATE P. 64 The renderings of the last judgment on papyri depict the deceased in the huge judgment-hall. The god Horus and the lord of the necropolis, Anubis, are shown weighing upon a pair of scales the symbol of the human heart in one pan; in the other pan is the symbol for 'truth'. Thoth, the ibis-headed god of wisdom, is recording the result. The god Osiris acts as judge.

Truth and justice — maat — are the yardstick by which men's conduct are judged.

The concept of the last judgment enhances the importance attached to the Osiris myth in the final phase of the Old Kingdom. During the Pyramid Period it was thought that the god-king alone would rise from the dead like the god Osiris. Now this concept is extended and applies to all men. The funerary inscriptions confirm this: the name of the god Osiris is placed before the name of the deceased. This formula, which degenerated into a *cliché*, demonstrates that the tendency towards spirituality implied in the Osiris myth, with its last judgment, was never quite able to efface the magic attitude basic to the Egyptians' way of thinking.

During the Middle Kingdom a general process of secularization seems to have resulted in a decline in the importance of religion in people's lives. The state relies more upon observance of ethical norms than divine sanctions. The unity of god and man, of the finite and the infinite world, has been lost — a consequence of the spiritual convulsions that led to the collapse of the Old Kingdom. The newly-established political order, and the spiritual basis on which it rests, necessitate a self-reliant and intellectual outlook rooted in philosophy rather than religion.

FIG. 23 — *Reconstruction of the pillared chapel of Sesostris I at Karnak. XIIth Dynasty, 1971-1930 B.C. Cf. p. 109.*

# VIII. ART AND ARCHITECTURE IN
THE MIDDLE KINGDOM

The few relics that remain of pharaonic architecture during the ARCHITECTURE
Middle Kingdom can give only an inadequate idea of the intensity
of power and austere simplicity that characterize the art of this period. *Temples*
Few temples have survived, since the monuments of the Middle Kingdom had to give way to the magnificent temples of the New Kingdom.
Often they were simply demolished and the stones used in the construction of new buildings. The relics that are left yield little information about the temples erected in honour of the gods by rulers of
the XIth Dynasty at Dendera, Thebes, Tod, Armant, Elephantine
and Abydos. Similarly, very few architectural remains have survived
from the XIIth Dynasty. It is known that temples existed at Bubastis,
Hermopolis, Abydos, Thebes and Medamut. At Heliopolis a granite
obelisk erected by Sesostris I recalls that a temple formerly stood there,
built by Amenemhat. Fortunately, at Karnak there were discovered,
built into a pylon dating from the reign of Amenophis III, the ar- FIG. 23
chitectural members of a jubilee chapel dedicated to Sesostris I. This
has been reconstructed. It was set on a raised platform and approached by ramps on the shorter sides, and contained a walled chamber.
This was surrounded by pillars, and these pillars were connected by
low balustrades.

A small chapel near Medinet Madi, in the Faiyum, dates from the FIG. 24
reigns of Amenemhat III and IV. It consists of a small portico, with

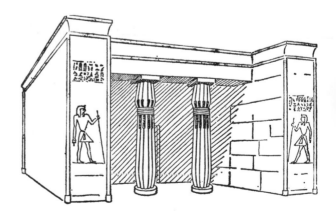

FIG. 24 — *Chapel of Amenemhat III and
IV, with papyrus-bundle columns, at Me-
dinet Madi. XIIth Dynasty, approx. 1790
B.C. Reconstruction. Cf. above*

two lotus-bundle columns, and another chamber, placed transversely, containing the chapels of the deities that were venerated there, arranged consecutively.

Of the royal tombs little has survived apart from the Mortuary Temple of Mentuhotep II. This magnificent terraced temple, erected in a deep bay in the cliffs on the western bank of the river at Thebes, in the region known as Deir el-Bahari, is an attempt to transplant the idea of the Old Kingdom pyramid tombs into a different milieu — the mountainous region around Thebes.

A broad causeway flanked by walls runs from the valley to the sheer mountain side. It leads into a court which is closed off at the western end by two colonnades. From this court another ramp leads to a terrace, on which stands the mortuary temple. It is surrounded on three sides by pillared porticos, which in turn terminate in a large hall containing octagonal pillars; above this rises the pyramid. To the west is an adjoining open court, enclosed by pillars, which gave access to the sepulchral chamber. The adjoining pillared hall, in front of a funerary chapel, is built into the cliff-face.

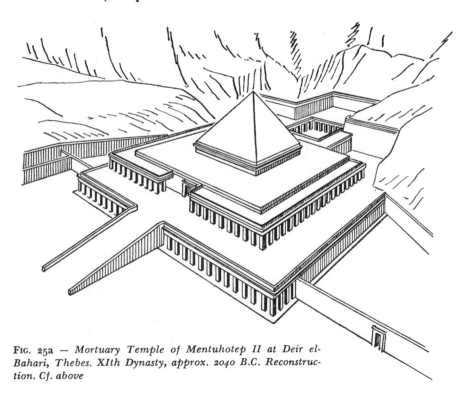

FIG. 25a — *Mortuary Temple of Mentuhotep II at Deir el-Bahari, Thebes. XIth Dynasty, approx. 2040 B.C. Reconstruction. Cf. above*

PLATE 31 — Limestone relief showing King Semenkhkara and his consort Meritaton promenading in the garden. New Kingdom, XVIIIth Dynasty, Amarna Period, approx. 1350 B.C. *Height 24 cm. Former National Museums, Berlin. Cf. p. 171.*

PLATE 32 — King Tutankhamun and his queen. Back support of the king's throne, from his tomb in the Valley of the Kings in the mountains at Thebes. Gilded wood with inlay of silver, faience and coloured enamel. New Kingdom, XVIIIth Dynasty, approx. 1340 B.C. *Egyptian Museum, Cairo. Diameter approx. 53 cm. Cf. p. 171.*

PLATE 33    Mural showing two daughters of Amenophis IV (Akhnaton). From the palace near the temple
dedicated to Aton, at Amarna. New Kingdom, XVIIIth Dynasty, Amarna Period, approx. 1350 B.C.
*Ashmolean Museum, Oxford. 30 x 41 cm. Cf. p. 171.*

PLATE 34 — Painted limestone statuette of Tetiseneb. New Kingdom, early XVIIIth Dynasty, approx. 1570 B.C. *Kestner Museum, Hanover. Height 30.8 cm. Cf. p. 174.*

This new type of construction, the work of Mentuhotep II, who united the 'Two Lands', combines the idea expressed in the pyramids with the rock-cut tomb traditional among nomarchs during the final phase of the Old Kingdom. This monument, the only one of its kind, is a testimony to the claims put forward by the new dynasty that it was the successor to the god-kings of the Pyramid Period. Abstract monumentality is translated into the symmetrical order and articulation of a less pretentious building, which adheres strictly to clarity of form and blends with its physical setting. In scale it is human rather than divine.

In lieu of the walls which, in the Mortuary Temple of King Chephren, shut off the chamber from the outside world, we have open pillared halls into which light can penetrate. The rites performed are thus made visible to onlookers. Columns in the form of plants — so popular during the Vth Dynasty — recede into the background completely. Square or octagonal pillars, with their sharply-defined lines, conform to the strictly rectilinear character of the building complex as a whole.

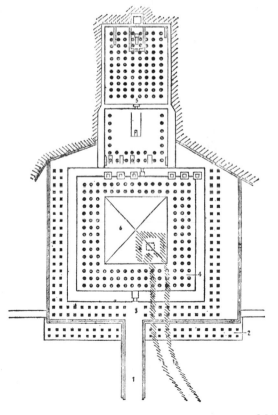

FIG. 25b — *Ground-plan of the Mortuary Temple of Mentuhotep II. Cf. p. 110.*
1. *Causeway*
2. *Lower colonnade*
3. *First terrace, with a pillared portico on three sides*
4. *Columned court*
5. *Hall with Holy of Holies, cut into the cliff*
6. *Pyramid*

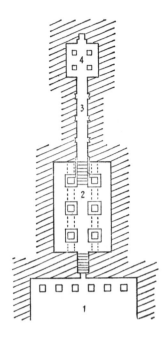

FIG. 26 — *Ground-plan of tomb of Prince Sarenput of Elephantine, at Aswan. XIIth Dynasty, approx. 1800 B.C. Cf. p. 118.*
1. *Forecourt with columns*
2. *Pillared hall*
3. *Corridor*
4. *Small pillared hall and chapel*

The rulers of the XIIth Dynasty moved their seat of government and place of residence back to Lower Egypt. The unpretentious pyramids and mortuary temples which they erected near Lisht and Dahshur, and near Hawara on the edge of the Faiyum, copy the design of Old Kingdom royal tombs.

The pyramids, which measured no more than some 50 to 60 metres in height, were built of sun-dried brick around a fan-shaped core of limestone. With their casing, also of limestone, they resembled the Great Pyramids of Giza.

*Private tombs*    During the Old Kingdom, when Lower Egypt, with its capital at Memphis, was the seat of government, the tombs of kings and court officials were built near the residence. By comparison with the extensive cemeteries at Giza and Sakkara the tombs in Upper Egypt, which was no more than a province, were much less important.

In the Middle Kingdom the scene is entirely different.

*Nomarchs' tombs*    The tombs of the feudal nobility, who attained an independent status towards the close of the Old Kingdom, were situated in their respective nomes. Thus the necropolis of the Theban nomarchs of the early XIth Dynasty is to be found north of the western bank of the Nile at Thebes. On the land that rises up gradually from the plain large forecourts have been excavated. In the rear wall of these are doorways, placed close together, which lead into the sepulchral chambers. The wall, broken by these rectangular openings, gives the impression of a pillared hall, which may subsequently have exerted an influence upon the development of rock-tombs. The rock-tombs of the nomarchs at Aswan and Meir followed the tradition of the tombs built here during the VIth Dynasty. During the first half of the XIIth Dynasty rock-tombs were also constructed by the nomarchs of Beni Hasan, El Bersha, Asyut and Qaw el-Kebir in their respective nomes. With the strengthening of the state power during the latter half of the XIIth Dynasty the importance of the feudal nobility declined. After the reign of Amenemhat III scarcely any nomarchs' tombs have survived except for the one at Qaw el-Kebir.

In the case of the tombs of the Elephantine princes in the mountain sanctuary at Aswan, the chambers are arranged in logical consecutive order, and the fine austere lines of the individual architectural mem-

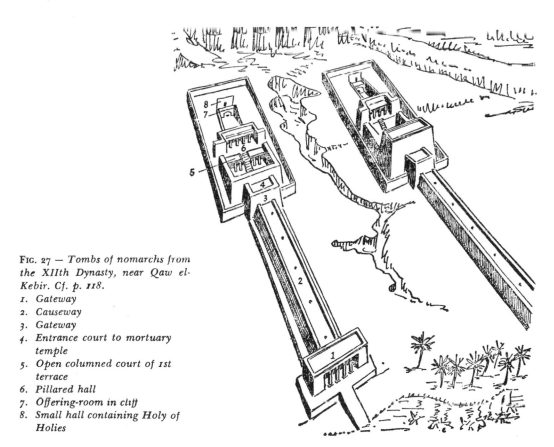

FIG. 27 — *Tombs of nomarchs from the XIIth Dynasty, near Qaw el-Kebir. Cf. p. 118.*
1. *Gateway*
2. *Causeway*
3. *Gateway*
4. *Entrance court to mortuary temple*
5. *Open columned court of 1st terrace*
6. *Pillared hall*
7. *Offering-room in cliff*
8. *Small hall containing Holy of Holies*

bers blend well with one another.

FIG. 26 The XIIth Dynasty tombs of Sarenput I and his grandson Sarenput II contain a pillared portico with an adjoining pillared hall. This leads to a barrel-vaulted corridor and finally terminates in an offering-room. At Beni Hasan the earliest tombs to which a date may be assigned were approached by an opening cut into the cliff-face, which was levelled off. This passage leads into a lavishly painted hall, divided by lotus-bundle columns. Beni Hasan added emphasis to the entrance by a small portico. As in the inner chambers, 16-sided pillars were used. They had round bases and were topped by square abacuses. On account of their faint resemblance to Doric columns they are referred to as 'proto-Doric'. Some of the tombs at Asyut consist simply of a large hall, without articulation.

FIG. 27 Most lavish in design are the tombs of the nomarchs of Qaw el-Kebir, dating from the latter half of the XIIth Dynasty. They are conceived as a combination of rock-tomb and mortuary temple. The tomb of Prince Wah-ka II, dating from the reign of Amenemhat III, has a gateway situated at the edge of the fertile strip of land, from which a ramp ascends through a second gateway to the pylon-like entrance to the mortuary temple, which is divided by slender 16-sided pillars. From the centre of the chamber a flight of steps leads to a terrace designed as an open hall, with two rows of papyrus-bundle columns. A ramp begins in front of the rear wall and leads to a pillared hall situated at a higher level. The adjoining chamber, used for the funerary cult, is cut into the cliff-face. There were niches carved in the wall which contained statues. A smaller hall behind this one was reserved for the funerary statue.

*Tombs of court officials* The rock-tombs of court officials from the XIth Dynasty are situated in the cliffs surrounding the Mortuary Temple of Mentuhotep II at Deir el-Bahari. Through a gateway, behind which the statue of the deceased was erected in a chapel, a path led half-way up the cliff. In some cases the entrance is accentuated by a pillared hall, from which a corridor decorated with reliefs runs to a chapel-like chamber containing the funerary statue. From this chamber a walled-up shaft led to the sarcophagus-chamber, situated at a lower level.

The new court nobility of the XIIth Dynasty had their burial-places built near the royal pyramids, as was the common practice in the Old Kingdom.

As was the case with the Cheops Pyramids, these tombs took the form of mastabas. In their interior there were neither reliefs nor statues.

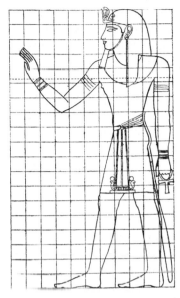

FIG. 28 — *Network of squaring lines used for drawing outlines of reliefs, used from the beginning of the Middle Kingdom onwards. Cf. p. 120.*

Even less frequent are simple shaft graves with no superstructure of any kind.

Only Intefiker, a court official who was vizier under Sesostris I, arranged to be buried in the mountains near Thebes, far from the capital. His tomb contained, in lieu of a pillared hall as in the nomarchs' tombs, a long corridor decorated with paintings. This led to the offering-room, whence it was possible to reach, by means of a shaft, the sarcophagus-chamber, which was situated at a lower level. In addition to these various types of Middle Kingdom tombs, there *Tombs in the Delta* are the simple underground tombs found in the region of the Delta, which contain no more than a single sarcophagus-chamber, and the tombs built of sun-dried brick with vaulted roofs in the western part of the Delta.

With the collapse of the Old Kingdom in internecine strife artistic **RELIEF AND** production gradually came to a standstill. Only individual nomarchs **PAINTING** in Upper Egypt kept up the custom of embellishing their tombs with reliefs and paintings. These are confused, both from the standpoint of style and of the techniques employed. Loud colours and clumsy crude forms show that the tradition of the Old Kingdom was now dead, and that the provincial craftsmen were endeavouring to formulate a new style — sometimes also to depict new subjects. Since Upper Egyptian artists lacked experience, and had no models to copy, they had to develop their talents completely afresh. An important aid

FIG. 28

FIG. 18

was provided by the introduction, at Thebes during the XIth Dynasty, of the system of drawing squaring lines on the surface of the stone. They fulfilled the same role as the units of measurement used in the Old Kingdom, and were an improvement on this system in that not only the general proportions, but every detail, could now be fixed precisely. This system of lines enabled a new artistic tradition to develop with surprising speed during the XIth Dynasty, which produced a symmetrical style of great beauty.

*Reliefs on royal monuments*

The earliest reliefs carved during the XIth Dynasty show that the artists were still groping in the dark. The figure appears raised, with little attempt at modelling and only sketchy inner markings, whereas the inscriptions are carved in sunk relief. But a tendency towards solidity of form is already heralded in the vigorous and lavishly painted reliefs, of which unfortunately only a few specimens have survived, from the Mortuary Temple of Mentuhotep II. In these the lines were drawn with elaborate care and a sure touch. They may be compared with the reliefs in the temples of Mentuhotep III at Tod, Armant and Elephantine; the latter are of particular elegance and delicacy, with exquisite figures worked in low relief.

To illustrate the reliefs of the early XIIth Dynasty we have a work showing Sesostris I performing a ritual dance before the god Min at Coptos, and also a relief on a pillar depicting the god Ptah embracing the king. The representation of the cult dance follows the scheme evolved during the Old Kingdom. A distinct difference between them

FIG. 29 — *Sesostris I and the god Ptah. Limestone relief on a pillar (detail). From Karnak. XIIth Dynasty, 1971-1930 B.C. Egyptian Museum, Cairo. Cf. p. 121.*

FIG. 30 — *Decorative inscription of Amenemhat III, from the temple of the crocodile-headed god Sobek at Crocodilopolis, in the Faiyum. Limestone. In the middle, between two standards depicting the god Sobek, is the royal title of Amenemhat III in the so-called cartouche (ring containing the name of the king). The two cartouches on either side contain his royal name. XIIth Dynasty, approx. 1840-1792 B.C. Berlin. Length 2.15 m. Cf. below*

and the earlier prototypes may be seen in the more heavily accentuated outlines of the sunk relief and the tendency to follow more closely the natural anatomy in the modelling. The motif of a close embrace, carved on the pillar in raised relief, opens up an entire FIG. 29 new world. In spite of the strictly symbolic treatment there is an inner relationship between the two figures. Around them are elaborately worked hieroglyphic signs, which give the composition as a whole an abstract decorative character.

The artistic way in which the writing and the figures are combined subsequently led to symmetrical compositions in which the two symbolic elements blended into a single homogeneous unit. The FIG. 30 individual hieroglyphs are executed with a closer eye to detail than was the case during the Old Kingdom. Instead of being merely marginal inscriptions, serving to explain the content of the picture and to make it magically effective, they now act as important 'sacred signs' — such as the Greeks understood them to be. The range of subjects treated in the paintings and reliefs on royal monuments is very limited. Typical of the solemn dignified style of the XIIth Dynasty are the precise arrangement of figures in the plane, the clear definition of the outlines, and the novel plastic modelling of the bodies.

The reliefs and paintings in the rock-tombs of the court nobility of *Reliefs and* the XIth Dynasty in the mountains near Thebes — of which only a *paintings in* few have survived — show that the superb style of the XIIth Dynasty *private tombs* had already been evolved by this time.

The pictures painted on stucco in the tomb of Intefiker [18] are also related stylistically to prototypes from the XIth Dynasty. Most of the scenes are concerned with the funerary ritual, but there are also other subjects, such as fishing, catching birds, crafts, agriculture and hunting. There are occasional departures from the practice of dividing up the plane evenly into registers. A bold and assured draughtsmanship is evident in the arrangement of the figures, which nevertheless still have a certain stiffness, as is clear when these scenes are compared with those painted at the same time in the nomarchs' tombs. To reach an assessment of the reliefs in the royal monuments and in the nobles' tombs we have only a few remains to guide us. In the case of the tombs of the nomarchs, on the other hand, there is a wealth of varied material.

In the rock-tombs that were built into the precipitous cliffs on the western and eastern banks of the Nile, especially in Middle Egypt, we have a local art form which, in spite of its conservative tendency, expresses many of the essential features of Middle Kingdom reliefs and paintings. In evaluating the decoration of these tombs the important factor is not so much their place in the chronological sequence of styles, as was the case with the Old Kingdom tombs, but the local tradition in the various nomes, each of which had its individual character.

F<small>IG</small>. 31 The subjects treated include, as in the Old Kingdom, the provisioning of the deceased, agriculture, cattle-raising, crafts and hunting. Occasionally we find simple copies of Vth Dynasty models. As well as obvious affinities with Old Kingdom reliefs, there are also links with those in the rock-tombs of court nobles from the XIth Dynasty at Thebes. But in the course of time completely new motifs came to be added.

The reliefs and paintings in the nomarchs' tombs are in keeping with the ostentatious character of the architecture, with its columned and

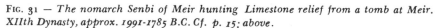

F<small>IG</small>. 31 — *The nomarch Senbi of Meir hunting Limestone relief from a tomb at Meir. XIIth Dynasty, approx. 1991-1785 B.C. Cf. p. 15; above.*

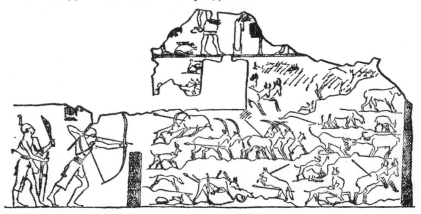

pillared halls. A novel assurance in the draughtsmanship can be seen in the disposition of the registers.

The principal function of the motifs used to embellish the tombs of the nomarchs is to glorify the prince as the ruler of his nome and to record the chief events in his life. The detailed cyclic representations on reliefs during the final phase of the Old Kingdom already gave a kaleidoscopic picture of life as it was lived in Egypt at the time. In the nomarchs' tombs of the Middle Kingdom there is a direct link with the contemporary world, since emphasis is occasionally laid on the uniqueness of the events depicted by giving the date when they took place. Thus in the tomb of Khnumhotep at Beni Hasan a Beduin prince is depicted accompanied by his retinue and seeking permission to settle in the nome. This memorable event, which it is doubtless the purpose of this mural to record, is ascribed by the accompanying inscription to the sixth year of King Sesostris II's reign.

FIG. 32

The scene showing a statue of the nomarch of El Bersha being transported to his offering-chapel is based on a unique event, to which such importance was attached that it was decided to record it for posterity. As the subjects became more and more secular, so also the purpose of the tombs underwent a change. They are no longer merely the 'eternal house' of the dead, but are designed to give posterity, through their pictorial representations, an idea of the services rendered by the nomarch.

Where the stone was suitable, as at El Bersha, Meir and Qaw el-Kebir, the decoration of the walls took the form of reliefs. At Beni Hasan the walls were coated with stucco and painted. From the XIIth Dynasty onwards paint acquires a new importance. Where it is applied freely and boldy over the plane, subtle shadings are possible that are not subject to any kind of schematic limitations. In representing flora and fauna a wide range of colours are evolved, following those found in nature, which blend harmoniously into one another. This provides evidence of a new relationship between man and nature. The landscape now forms a background or framework for the action depicted. The design of wall scenes seems to develop unimpaired by traditional rules laid down in workshops. Many and varied are the attempts made to render the human body in the most diverse phases of movement. The wrestling match depicted in a series of detailed pictures at Beni Hasan [19] offered ample opportunity for experimentation. The artist was able to produce an impression of depth in space by means of overlapping, foreshortening and representing figures viewed from an oblique angle, and also to portray a group of persons in a meaningful relationship to one another.

The state of preservation of the wall-paintings in the nomarchs' tombs is unfortunately very poor, and there is little left from the latter half of the XIIth Dynasty. But in the wooden sarcophagus of Prince Thotnakht [20] from El Bersha, dating from the reign of Sesostris III, we have an exquisite painting which shows the prince receiving incense in front of various funerary offerings.

The paint has been applied directly to the wood, without a slip underneath, and there are no preliminary outlines to indicate the shape of the figure to be painted. The delicate shadings of colour help to produce firm contour lines.

*Stelae* One special group of Middle Kingdom monuments must not remain unmentioned. The commercial classes, who for the first time were now acquiring a certain importance, have left an abundance of fu- PLATE P. 65 nerary stelae. Most of them originate from Abydos, where they were put up near the temple dedicated to Osiris. The pictures and inscriptions on these memorial tablets are designed to serve the deceased and his family in the after-life, but at the same time are monuments recalling his pilgrimage to Abydos and his acts of piety there. Thus the inscription conveys information about events during his life, frequently giving exact dates, and requests to the passer-by to say a prayer for the deceased. From an artistic point of view the quality of these commemorative tablets varies greatly; they offer a wealth of material that can help to arrive at a general evaluation of paintings and reliefs in the Middle Kingdom.

A study of the varied course taken by these branches of art during this period shows distinctly that images are losing their magic purpose and coming to depict conditions in this earthly world, at a particular place and time. What began as a symbol is becoming a likeness, a monument designed for human eyes. The range of themes conforms to the new significance attached to these images. So, too, does the

style, which is free and far removed from the schematic regimentation imposed by the artistic workshops. In reliefs executed in this style the human figure is elaborately modelled, and the details are clearly shown; they are harmoniously combined to form a whole. In paintings the themes are drawn from a wide range of colourful natural phenomena.

Old Kingdom sculpture, erected in royal mortuary temples or the statue-chambers of private tombs, was conceived as the abode of *ka*, man's immortal substance.

**SCULPTURE IN THE ROUND**

As a timeless idealized picture of the deceased, together with the inscriptions bearing his name, it was an embodiment of the deceased's expectations of a life beyond the grave. As well as funerary sculpture there was temple sculpture, which served to represent the king at festive rites. Neither of these types of sculpture were designed for human eyes, but they fulfilled their functions by the very fact of their existence. During the Vth and the VIth Dynasties the artistic form gradually began to approximate to that found in nature, and thus the austere character of the block-statue was broken. In consequence the meaning of the statue also changed. It became a monument to commemorate the deceased, designed for human eyes.

This change of meaning took place during the Middle Kingdom. It implied a modification of artistic style and of the way in which the figures were erected. In addition to funerary sculpture, there now appears temple sculpture that is distinctly commemorative in character.

The XIth Dynasty, coming after the turbulent period between the Old and Middle Kingdoms, consciously sought to follow the models of the Pyramid Period. Efforts were made to express in statuary the idea of royal power, which, despite the conditions of the time, was to possess the glory of the ancient sacrosanct monarchy.

The first attempt of an artist at Thebes to express the power of the new state is the statue of Mentuhotep II, who is depicted larger than life, clad in a jubilee cloak, with powerful legs and a massive compactness of form. As in the Pyramid Period, the basic form is a cubist one, with the planes meeting at right angles. The clarity and austerity of form that emerged at the beginning of the XIth Dynasty constitutes

FIG. 33

the starting-point from which royal sculpture rapidly evolved, in a direction that corresponded to the mood of the time.

In the colossal statue of Amenemhat I from Tanis, which measures some 2.68 metres in height, we encounter a pharaoh of the early XIIth Dynasty. He is shown seated upon a block-shaped throne, with a ledge for his feet and a low supporting back-pillar. The body, with the hands shown resting on the thigh, is modelled with assurance and precision. The face is worked in detail and appears far more animated than is the case with the Mentuhotep statue. An impression of magnanimous dignity is evoked by the slightly curving lines of cosmetic paint, the soft modelling of the mouth, and the contemplative eyes. This statue used to stand in one of the open temple courts, suffused by the bright sunlight. The people assembled in the temple court saw in this statue their ruler, the representative of the state power. The different meaning now attached to temple sculpture is the result of the change that has occurred in the concept of monarchy. The ruler of the new state is no longer the god-king of the Pyramid Period, but a human being. His authority is based, not upon divine sanction, but on ethical norms. Like other men, he is subject to the will of fate and to temporal laws. We possess colossal statues of Sesostris I from his mortuary temple at Lisht,[21] which were used in the funerary cult of the king. They follow the traditional form of the funerary statue. The animated face, modelled with an eye to detail, distinguishes it from the Old Kingdom cult statues. The so-called Osiride pillars represent the king in the guise of a mummified Osiris, leaning against a pillar.

*Sphinges* Two sphinges of Amenemhat II, made of red Aswan granite, are known; they were discovered at Tanis.[22] The curved lines of the lion's body are effectively combined with the head of the king, with deep eye-sockets and grooves to suggest wrinkles, and framed by the royal head-dress. It gives the impression of an ancient sphinx, but in a novel guise. In the case of the sphinx of Amenemhat II the head-dress, draped in an artistic manner, forms the link between the animal body and human head. In the case of the sphinges with manes of Amenemhat III, which were also discovered at Tanis, the king's face is not emphasized in this way by the head-dress; instead, it is framed

Fig. 34

Plate p. 66

FIG. 35 — *Brown sandstone statue of Khertihotep,*
*from Asyut (?). XIIth Dynasty, 1991-1785 B.C. Ber-*
*lin. Height 75 cm. Cf. p. 128.*

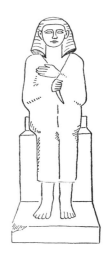

by the lion's mane. The only parts that have survived are the uraeus serpent and the royal beard below the chin. Here, too, the king and the lion form a composite whole: the body is that of the majestic king of the desert, and above this there rises the head of the ruler, whose countenance suggests both energy and composure.

Under Sesostris II the image of the king gains in depth and content. The hollows at the corners of the mouth and the broad upper eyelids indicate that a further step has now been taken towards portraiture — the portrait of a man with spiritual qualities.

It is in the reigns of Sesostris III and Amenemhat III that sculptors finally come to carve men's features in such a way as to express the personality of the individual concerned, as a temporal being.

At the beginning of the XIIth Dynasty, in faces which portrayed Amenemhat I and Sesostris I, the old eternally valid conventions were still followed, but with Sesostris III all the lines and individual sculpted volumes are shown in movement. High cheek-bones and eyebrows emphasize the bone structure of the face. The upper lids of the eyes hang down heavily; the dynamic narrow mouth, firm chin and flabby cheeks; the lines around the top of the nose and the lachrymal bags under the eyes — all these features combine to produce a likeness of shattering expressive force. The plastically modelled individual parts of the face suggest spiritual tension. The result is the vital image of a ruler conscious of the transitoriness of worldly things. The royal heads of the Pyramid Period were images of manhood in its prime — the product of a belief in the timeless existence of the god-king. By the end of the Middle Kingdom they have given way to images of men stricken by doubt. They seem to be conscious of their spiritual isolation and the heavy responsibilities that lie upon them. The likenesses of Amenemhat III reflect solemn majesty, and the melancholy of a man who sees the political and spiritual order in danger of imminent collapse.

After twenty years of turbulence the princely family from Gebelein in Upper Egypt came to power as the XIIIth Dynasty and attempted to bring about an artistic renaissance. The excellent technique displayed in a number of colossal statues of these rulers, situated at Tanis, cannot, however, conceal the fact that the forms are rigid and

PLATE P. 83

*XIIIth Dynasty*

the expression vacant, lacking in spiritual tension.

Old Kingdom sculpture originates almost exclusively from the environs of Memphis. When one turns to the Middle Kingdom, one has to take into consideration the Delta area, Lisht and Thebes. The colossal figures and sphinges originating from Tanis, in the Delta, are as a rule made of hard black granite and display great pathos.

In evaluating statuary importance must be attached not only to the chronology of stylistic development, which may be followed clearly in the royal figures, but also to the distinction between funerary and temple statues, and to the place of origin.

*Sculpture of private persons*  Little has survived in the way of figures of private persons, as distinct from royal figures.

So far as funerary statues from nomarchs' tombs are concerned, only fragments have been preserved — and from the reign of Amenemhat III onwards even these are lacking. The mastaba tombs and shaft graves of the court nobility of the XIIth Dynasty were too small for funerary statues.

Already towards the close of the Old Kingdom a decree of Pepi II gave a vizier, as an exception, permission to erect a statue of himself in the temple. A royal decree dating from the First Intermediate Period, which testifies to the growing importance of the commercial classes, reveals that the king allowed private individuals to erect such statues in the temple, and also helped to maintain them by making *Temple sculpture* food offerings and causing rites to be performed. These temple statues can hardly be regarded as monuments to glorify the dead, as is the case with the royal figures. They afford the deceased the opportunity to partake in the cult performed in the temple, and to receive the prayers of visitors.

The style of private sculpture bears a resemblance to that of the royal figures of this era.

From the XIth Dynasty we have a number of statuettes which in their crude vigour are heralds of a new artistic form. Others follow Old Kingdom traditions. During the early XIIth Dynasty a new style evolves in the carving of figures of private persons, as of royal statuary. In contrast to the *joie de vivre* expressed in the Old Kingdom statues, this style suggests austere and dignified majesty. Men are *Cloaked figures* depicted clad in a long kilt that reaches down from the waist or chest *Fig. 35* to the ankles, or alternatively cloaked in a garment covering the whole figure. Characteristic are the voluminous forms. The general impression is governed by the plastically modelled face.

The artist makes the garment part of the composition: beneath it the bodily forms can be made out. In the Old Kingdom statues, on the other hand, the garment was not distinguished from the silhouette of the body. The draping of the cloak and occasional flaring of the hem contrive to suggest the texture of the garment in question. The austere compactness of the cloaked figures is found in a more intensified form in the cube-shaped statue. This feature accorded absolutely with the character of Egyptian art, and continued to exert an influence right up to the Late Period. The cube-shaped statue is the PLATE P. 131 final and most obvious demonstration of the principle that prevailed from the Pyramid Period onwards: the encompassing of the plastic figure within the rectangular planes of the cube or pillar. The figure is depicted clad in a cloak, squatting with knees drawn up; the back and lower part of the leg form a vertical plane. Only the head, and occasionally also the feet and hands (shown crossed over the knees), are outside the limits of this cubist form. The concentration upon the geometric element, into which the organic human figure is blended, does not, however, give an impression of rigidity or abstractness; on the contrary, the planes of the cube follow the silhouette of the body, conveying the organic character of the squatting figure. Here naturalistic and abstract style are combined in such a way as to produce a balanced and homogeneous whole.

The close of the Middle Kingdom saw the carving of the black granite *XIIIth Dynasty* statue of Sebekemsaf, who was related to the ruling house under the XIIIth Dynasty; it measures some 1.50 metres in height. The perfec- FIG. 36 tion of the technique employed in working the hard and smoothly polished stone cannot conceal the fact that there is a certain rigidity about the way in which the forms of the figure are built up. The arms are held tightly to the body, and the long protruding kilt is depicted in a stiff manner. Although the realistic modelling of the face under the XIIth Dynasty was never employed when treating the body, the statue of Sebekemsaf also renders his corpulent figure. The heavily lined face has become a mask behind which it is no longer possible to detect any spiritual feeling.

Rigid formalism is characteristic of spiritual decline. Its traces become ever more evident in XIIIth Dynasty works.

Were Middle Kingdom sculptures painted? The question cannot be answered for certain on the basis of the colossal statues that have survived, which are not painted. It may be assumed that paint was applied to funerary sculpture, which followed the Old Kingdom tradition and used limestone as the principal medium. Temple sculpture, and especially the colossi of hard stone discovered at Tanis, on the other hand, show that the sculptors had a distinct sense for the naturalistic effect produced by the stone. Apart from this, the fine plastic modelling of details makes it doubtful whether the statues were painted. It may be that artists did not go further in this direction than occasional inlaying of eyes with different coloured materials, and the use of paint to denote jewellery, crown and hair.

This survey of Middle Kingdom art may be concluded with a reference to the wealth of small carvings in stone, faience, wood and bronze, often treated in a highly realistic manner.

PLATE P. 84

Painted wooden statuettes, servant figurines and models of granaries, kitchens, boats and armed soldiers continue in the tradition established at the close of the Old Kingdom. Their artistic quality varies greatly.

PLATE P. 87.

In some of them, such as the XIIth Dynasty statuette of Imeret-nebes, there is an expression of austere and dignified composure which is characteristic of large-scale sculpture at this time. Plastically modelled figurines of — for example — acrobats, dancers, wrestlers, apes, hippopotamuses and mice testify to the delight taken in searching out the most astonishing variety of motifs. We need not assume that there was any relationship between this rich popular form of art and funerary rites. They were made for the sake of their curious motifs, simply for their intrinsic value.

*Jewellery*

PLATE P. 86

Among the most outstanding achievements of Middle Kingdom art are the works produced by goldsmiths. With their exquisite well-blended colours and forms, they testify to the high level of technical expertise and the refined sense of form that existed in this era. Diadems and pectorals are singled out for especially lavish embellishment. Semi-precious stones such as cornelian, amethyst, lapis lazuli, turquoise and jasper are used for inlaying, and give these objects a colourful attractive aspect.

Ceramic ware was used for everyday purposes. No elaborate care was taken either with its form or its decoration. There are bulging ointment jars with flat lids, made of alabaster, and either white and yellow or grey and blue in colour. For ceremonial vessels of particular value obsidian was used.

FIG. 36 — *Black granite statue of Sebekemsaf from Armant. XIIIth Dynasty, approx. 1785-1660 B.C. Museum of Fine Arts, Vienna. Height 1.50 m. Cf. p. 129.*

PLATE 35 — Quartz block-statue of Senmut — one of the most influential court officials of Queen Hatshepsut, who was her 'minister of finance' as well as tutor to Princess Nefrure. New Kingdom, XVIIIth Dynasty, approx. 1490-1470 B.C. *British Museum. Height 54 cm. Cf. pp. 129, 175.*

PLATE 36 — Head of a statuette of Queen Tiy, a commoner who became the consort of Amenophis III. Painted yew-tree wood, gold and inlays. From Medinet Gurob, in the Faiyum. New Kingdom, XVIIIth Dynasty, approx. 1360 B.C. *Former National Museums, Berlin. Height 10.7 cm. Cf. p. 176.*

PLATE 37 — Princess, apparently from Amarna. Painted limestone. New Kingdom, late XVIIIth Dynasty, approx. 1340 B.C. *Louvre, Paris. Height 15 cm. Cf. p. 185.*

PLATE 38 — Bust of Queen Nefertiti, consort of Amenophis IV (Akhnaton). Painted limestone model. From Amarna. New Kingdom, XVIIIth Dynasty, Amarna Period, 1363-1343 B.C. *Former National Museums, Berlin. Height 50 cm. Cf. p. 185.*

PLATE 39 — Stucco mask of a royal official. From Amarna. New Kingdom, XVIIIth Dynasty, Amarna Period, approx. 1350 B.C. *Former National Museums, Berlin. Height 27 cm. Cf. p. 185.*

PLATE 41 — View of a court in the Ramesseum (the Mortuary Temple of Ramses II), on the western bank of the river at Thebes, containing colossi of the king. New Kingdom, XXth Dynasty, approx. 1198-1167 B.C.

*Cf. p. 189.*

◀ PLATE 40 — Detail of the ceiling in the Great Hall of the tomb of Seti I, in the Valley of the Kings at Thebes. New Kingdom, XIXth Dynasty, approx. 1300 B.C.

PLATE 42 — Entrance to the rock temple of Ramses II at Abu Simbel. New Kingdom, XIXth Dynasty, approx. 1250 B.C. *Cf. pp. 189, 199.*

PLATE 43 — The deceased worshipping the god Osiris. Fragment of a sarcophagus from Thebes. New Kingdom, XXth Dynasty, approx. 1100 B.C. *Rijksmuseum van Oudheden, Leyden. Cf. p. 197.*

PLATE 44 — Colossal limestone statue of Ramses II in the temple at Luxor, Thebes. New Kingdom, XIXth Dynasty, 1290-1224 B.C. *Cf. p. 200.*

PLATE 45 — Upper part of the gold sarcophagus of Tutankhamun. From his tomb in the Valley of the ▶ Kings, in the mountains at Thebes. New Kingdom, XVIIIth Dynasty, approx. 1340 B.C. *Egyptian Museum, Cairo. Total length of sarcophagus 1.85 m. Cf. p. 207.*

PLATE 46 — Faience bowl showing maiden sitting in a boat beneath hanging blossoms and playing an instrument. New Kingdom, XVIIIth Dynasty, approx. 1370 B.C. *Rijksmuseum van Oudheden, Leyden. Diameter 12 cm. Cf. p. 207.*

# IX. THE NEW KINGDOM

The New Kingdom was an era when Egypt, now a world power, HISTORICAL SURVEY waged wars of conquest against its neighbours. They began with the expulsion of the Hyksos. The Theban princely family, which had risen to power in Upper Egypt at a time when the Hyksos held sway over Lower Egypt, gradually extended their influence northwards. After many years of indecisive fighting King Ahmose succeeded in finally liberating Egypt from foreign domination. He is the first ruler of the XVIIIth Dynasty. His son Amenophis I and the latter's successor XVIIIth Dynasty Thutmosis I were faced with the task of quelling several rebellions in Nubia as well as the reorganization of the state. Thutmosis I managed to extend Egyptian power as far as the Fourth Cataract near Napata. During the five centuries that comprise the New Kingdom Napata remained the southern border of Egypt. MAP P. 235
The administration of the province of Nubia was entrusted to a governor who bore the title 'Son of the King of Kush' (Kush = Nubia). After order had been imposed on the south the king undertook a campaign to Palestine and Syria.
After the short reign of Thutmosis II feuding broke out between members of the Thutmosid dynasty, in the course of which Queen Hatshepsut acceded to the throne. Her step-brother and husband, Hatshepsut Thutmosis III, who had laid claim to the throne himself, had to be content with the relatively minor role of prince consort. During Hatshepsut's reign the country enjoyed peace and prosperity. Instead of marauding campaigns there were peaceful expeditions to Punt on the Somali coast.
After her reign, which lasted for nearly twenty years, Thutmosis III Thutmosis III succeeded in deposing his wife and winning the throne himself. Immediately afterwards he set out for Palestine, and near Megiddo defeated the combined forces of the princes who ruled the cities of Syria and Palestine. An alliance with the powerful kingdom of Mitanni led to the Near East becoming divided into two rival spheres of influence.
Egypt owed its acknowledged supremacy in the Near East to Thutmosis III's outstanding talents as a general and as a politician. His son, Amenophis II, consolidated its hold over Palestine and Syria.

Thutmosis IV, his successor, renewed the alliance with the kingdom of Mitanni, which was threatened by the rising power of the Hittites. He sealed the compact by marrying a Mitannian princess.

*Amenophis III*

When Amenophis III came to the throne he found the state firmly established both internally and externally. During his reign Egypt could enjoy years of untroubled glory. The proceeds of her flourishing commerce and the tribute she received from vanquished enemies ensured the land on the Nile considerable prosperity. Amenophis III's consort, Queen Tiy, was a commoner. Their son, Ameno-

*Amenophis IV (Akhnaton)*

phis IV — Akhnaton, as he later called himself after the sun-god Aton, whose worship he introduced — has left his mark on history as 'the heretical king of Amarna'. Important as his reign was for Egyptian religion and art, from a political point of view it marked the beginning of the gradual decline of the New Kingdom. While the king dedicated himself to his studies of religion and philosophy in his new residence at Amarna, surrounded by foreign mercenaries and a few loyal courtiers, the valuable territories in Palestine and Syria fell to the assaults of the Hittites and Amorites. In internal affairs, too, Akhnaton's 13-year reign resulted in dissension and unrest. The priests of the Temple of Amun at Karnak gradually arrogated to themselves an unhealthy degree of spiritual and material power. Meanwhile in the Delta the military leaders who were responsible for defending the country and protecting its Asiatic provinces were coming to enjoy considerable prestige and to play an important role in affairs. Thus on one hand the authority of the priests, officials and soldiers was growing, whereas that of the monarchy was weakening and becoming secularized .

*Tutankhamun*

After the death of Akhnaton his sons-in-law, Semenkhkara and Tutankhamun, in turn succeeded to the throne of the pharaohs. They were followed by Eye, an elderly courtier from the old residence at Amarna. Political conditions in the Near East were becoming steadily more troubled and posed a serious threat to the country's security. Syria had regained its independence, and Palestine, under pressure from the Beduins of the desert, appealed to Egypt for military protection.

In this time of weakness a powerful individual appeared on the scene in the person of Horemheb. He took the destinies of the country into his hands and thereby averted the threat of disintegration. Horemheb had his residence at Memphis, whence he sought to give support to the hard-pressed Palestinians. After the death of Eye he assumed the throne, becoming the first ruler of the XIXth Dynasty. His successor, Ramses I, was likewise a renowned general. His son, Seti I, continued the reconquest of Palestine and Syria which Horemheb had initiated. He fought the Hittites and also repelled attacks on Egypt's western borders by the Libyans.

Ramses II, who followed his father Seti on the throne, defeated the *Ramses II* Hittites in the celebrated battle at Kadesh in Syria without, however, defeating them decisively. As a result of an alliance with Hattusil, king of the Hittites, the Near East was divided up once more into rival spheres of influence, Egyptian and Hittite. The friendly relations between the two empires were consolidated by vigorous trade links and the marriage of Ramses II to the eldest daughter of King Hattusil.

Under the XIXth Dynasty Egypt's capital was at Tanis in the Delta. The Near East and Mediterranean were, however, to remain sources of trouble for a long time to come. Under Merneptah, son of Ramses II, the towns along the Mediterranean coast were harassed by the 'Peoples of the Sea', among whom were Achaeans, Philistines, Tyrsenians and Sherden. During the XXth Dynasty the peace of the border was constantly being disturbed by enemy attacks and the immigration of alien settlers. Under the second king of the XXth Dynasty, *XXth Dynasty;* Ramses III, the last of the mighty rulers of the New Kingdom, the *Ramses III* Egyptians once again succeeded in repelling the Libyans in the west and protecting the security of their eastern borders, in a great naval battle against the pressure of the migrants, to which the Hittite empire fell victim. After the assassination of Ramses III the kings rapidly lost their power and the unity of the country was again disrupted. During this period the power of the High Priest of the Temple of Amun increased. This office had become hereditary under Ramses IV. The High Priest Herihor, who was simultaneously also governor of Nubia, took over control of Upper Egypt, while Smendes ruled the Delta as successor to the Ramsessids.

During the ensuing XXIst Dynasty attempts were made to bring *XXIst Dynasty* about a political unification of the two dynasties by marriage. But this was achieved only under the XXIInd Dynasty, the rulers of which were descendants of a Libyan officer who had settled at Herakleopolis, in the northern part of Upper Egypt, in the Ramessid era.

The XXIInd Dynasty, which had its seat of government at Bu- *Libyan rule;* bastis in the Delta, ruled the country for 200 years. To break the *XXIInd XXIIIrd* threatening power of the Amun priests, the office of High Priest of *Dynasties*

Amun was invested in a prince of royal blood. When order had been restored at home, an attempt was made to regain control of Palestine. A princely family from the Delta ruled the country as the XXIIIrd Dynasty.

Towards the end of the period of Libyan domination Egypt once again split into petty principalities. One of the most important of them was Tanis in the Delta. Prince Tefnakhte of Saïs and his son Bocchoris are reckoned as the XXIVth Dynasty. Their attempts to unite the whole country were threatened by the invading Nubians, who had occupied Thebes already during the XXIIIrd Dynasty. The rule of the Nubians (Ethiopians) marks the beginning of the Late Period of Egyptian culture.

*Tefnakhte of Saïs*

The princes from Thebes who were responsible for the expulsion of the Hyksos and the unification of Egypt owed their claim to the throne of the pharaohs to their forceful intervention in the destinies of the country. To ensure the position of the monarchy they took a number of measures, among which was the revival of the old dogma to the effect that the king was the son of god. This concept was, however, interpreted in a different manner from that current in Old Kingdom times. During the New Kingdom the queen was regarded as the 'divine wife of Amun'. Amun himself, the king of gods, assumes the person of the king and fathers the successor to the throne, who can thus trace his claim directly to the national god Amun. Queen Hatshepsut had this event represented in her mortuary temple at Deir el-Bahari.

*Monarchy*

In his daily life the king abides by earthly laws, unaffected by his claim to divinity. He is both god and man. This becomes particularly evident during the golden age of the New Kingdom, when Amenophis III marries a commoner, or in the Amarna figures. The latter depict the king surrounded by his family, with all his bodily weaknesses and deformities reproduced.

During the campaigns fought by the Thutmosids a rigidly hierarchical political system evolved, resting upon military commanders and administrative officials. It was headed by two viziers who had their seats of government at Memphis and Thebes. The nobility ceased to play an important role. The princes of El Kab were the only ones who continued to exercise a certain influence until the beginning of the XVIIIth Dynasty.

*Administrative system*

During the New Kingdom the army, which in the hands of the pharaohs was a far from negligible factor in the political situation, also enrolled foreign mercenaries. They were settled in the country and towards the close of the New Kingdom became a threat to the authority of the state, which by that time was greatly weakened.

In the administration, too, there was an excessive amount of foreign influence owing to the employment of immigrants. This was why the Libyans succeeded so easily in winning control once the state had disintegrated.

As well as the monarchy, army and bureaucracy an important and dangerous part was played by the priesthood of the Temple of Amun at Karnak. The massive temple complex, which had been erected to the national god Amun, stood on the eastern embankment of the Nile at Thebes. Many bequests were made to it, and the priests who administered these riches were eventually able to acquire considerable power. They formed, so to speak, a state within the state, interfering in worldly matters and setting themselves up in opposition to the monarchy. The pharaohs of the XIXth Dynasty, who resided in the Delta, exercised but little influence upon developments at Thebes. Under Ramses III the Thebaïd enjoyed almost complete independence. When the office of High Priest of Amun became hereditary, under Ramses IV, the basis was provided for a concentration of religious and political power in their hands. The plentiful tribute he received from Nubia and his establishment of an armed force of his own enabled the High Priest Herihor to make his bid for supreme power. He was also governor of Nubia and vizier of Upper Egypt.

*Priesthood*

Both religion and ritual played a far more important role in the New Kingdom than they had in the Middle Kingdom. The determination on the part of the new dynasty to consolidate its political power by attaching supreme significance to a local god at Thebes led to the Amun cult centred on that city. In the Old Kingdom Amun appears as the personification of 'the hidden (god)' in the Hermopolitan doctrine of creation. At Thebes he appears in human guise, wearing a double plumed crown. The Amun cult was not a new religion but was pieced together from earlier religious notions. Amun now takes pride of place in the hierarchy of deities. Theologians identify him with the sun-god Rē and the Great God of Memphis, Ptah.

RELIGION

*Amun cult*

In this interpretation he appears as Amun-Rē, king of the gods. Together with the sun-god Rē the whole Heliopolitan pantheon moved to Thebes, and with Ptah all the gods of Memphis did so too. In order to ensure Amun's hegemony over the gods of the various nomes and localities, it was said that he was the oldest deity and that through him all the other gods had come into being. In a hymn to Amun the following lines occur:

> 'More orderly [ancient] is Thebes than any other city. The water and the land were in her in the beginning of time, and the creation of the world and the gods happened at Thebes under its god Amun.' 23

It was the Amun cult that led to the building of the gigantic national temple at Karnak, a task which absorbed the energies of several generations. The Egyptian word for Karnak is *ipet-iset,* or 'counter of the places' — i.e., the assembly-place of all the Egyptian deities, who as 'visiting gods' had their chapels in the national temple, where they were worshipped.

Amun-Rē is the god of the living, the mighty king of all the gods in the Egyptian empire. There never existed a religious dogma with its own specific content, which developed the concept of the god's effectiveness, qualities or commandments. The name Amun, 'the hidden (god)', may perhaps designate the one supreme god who was already referred to in earlier days as 'he with the hidden name', the god who controlled all knowledge and experience.

The theology behind the Amun religion and the ritual festivals associated with it are closely bound up with the monarchy and served to enhance its power. An attempt was made to bring the national god closer to the people by representing him in animal as well as human guise — as a fam with twisted horns, or as a goose. However, such efforts were foredoomed to failure. The masses adhered to their ancient local deities, whose places of worship had existed in the townships and nomes for centuries, and in particular to Osiris, who played a crucial part as ruler over the realm of the dead. While the theologians wrestled with the problems of presenting God as Spirit, the people clung more firmly than ever to their belief in magic. It is this magical outlook that explains their concern to provide for the deceased in the after-life, when he was deemed to have risen again as Osiris. As in olden times the body was mummified and the viscera buried separately in four canopic jars, which were under the protection of the spirits of the dead. The funerary offerings of the deceased included, as well as a lavish supply of furniture and jewellery, amulets and servant figurines. The Book of the Dead, written on papyrus and placed in the sarcophagus, was designed to provide protection against all the dangers which the deceased might encounter on his journey into the nether world.

*Popular beliefs*

PLATE P. 85

148

In spite of the magnificent temples and the vast number of cult festivals, which were celebrated on a lavish scale, religion seems to lose its *élan*. This was the consequence of the firm bond that existed between religious teaching and the power of the state, and the enhanced importance given to ritual.

Amenophis IV, who acceded to the throne of the pharaohs in 1377 B.C., was bold enough to attempt a comprehensive reform, by substituting a new faith for the multiplicity of beliefs current in Egypt at the time. According to this new religion Aton, the sun's disc visible in the sky, is the sole god. Already in the Old Kingdom the sun's disc was called 'Aton', although this did not denote a specific person. As inscriptions and literary texts show, shortly before Amenophis IV came to the throne there was a more pronounced tendency in favour of worshipping the sun-god Rē who, as a cosmic deity, exerted more influence upon people's lives than the state god Amun. *Aton cult*

The sun-god Rē of Heliopolis lost the supremely important position that he had held in the Vth Dynasty. The deities worshipped in the individual nomes were represented with the qualities of Rē, and frequently even bore his name as well, in order to lend weight to their claim to universal significance. In this way the specific content of the sun-cult was lessened. It may at first have been Amenophis IV's intention to free the sun-cult from the false interpretations and ambiguities that had accumulated over the centuries and to clarify the nature of the sun-god. The particular veneration which the king accorded to the sun-god, and his concern for truth, were already evident from the name he took at his accession: 'he who is living in truth, the only one of Rē'.

The royal reformer expressed his religious ideas in the title he gave the sun-god: 'Long live Rēhorakhty, who rejoices on the horizon in his name of Shu, who is Aton'. This phrase contains the names by which the sun-god had been worshipped since ancient times. Rēhorakhty is the falcon-headed sun-god in the teaching of Heliopolis, who makes his appearance shining on the horizon, where the sun rises and sets. Shu, god of the air, symbolizes the link between the celestial disc and the earth, whereas Aton denotes the celestial body itself. After some time the falcon-headed sun-god is superseded by the image of the sun's round disc, whose rays terminate in hands holding the symbol of life. In this way the mythological interpretation and ancient tradition of the Heliopolitan doctrine gave way to worship of the sun as the life-giving and life-sustaining force. FIG. 79

During the sixth year of his reign Amenophis IV moved his residence to Amarna to escape from the priests of Amun at Thebes, who were putting up resistance to the new doctrine. At Amarna he had a separate temple built in honour of Aton. At the same time he changed his name Amenophis ('Amun is satisfied') to Akhnaton ('Pleasing to Aton') and thus brought about a final breach with the official state religion and the Theban priesthood.

At Amarna the king gave an interpretation of his new concept of the deity by re-formulating the title of the sun-god: 'Rē, Lord of the two horizons, who rejoices on the horizon, lives in his name of Rē the Father, who has appeared as Aton'. The name of Rēhorakhty, another form of the sun-god, and that of the god Shu no longer occur in this interpretation. But the sun-god Rē appears as the ancient Great God, who existed from the very dawn of time and who appears to man in the guise of his son Aton. It is surprising that Akhnaton, having elucidated his concept of the deity in this way, by paraphrasing his name, did not attempt to substantiate his doctrine by evolving a dogma. The content of the new religion can be ascertained from prayers and songs which, however, do not add up to a theology.

*'Hymn to the Sun'* The famous 'Hymn of the King to the Sun' is a poem that describes the all-embracing power of the sun:

> 'Beautiful is thine appearing in the horizon of heaven,
> thou living sun, the first who lived!
> Thou risest in the eastern horizon,
> and fillest every land with thy beauty.
> Thou art beautiful and great, and glistenest,
> and art high above every land.
> Thy rays, they encompass the lands,
> so far as all that thou hast created.
> When thou goest down in the western horizon,
> the earth is in darkness, as if it were dead.
> When it is dawn and thou risest in the horizon
> and shinest as the sun in the day,
> thou dispellest the darkness and sheddest thy beams.
> The Two Lands keep festival and awake.
> All beasts are content with their pasture,
> the trees and the bushes are verdant.
> The birds fly out of their nests and their wings
> praise thy *ka*.

All wild beasts dance on their feet, all that fly
and flutter — they live when thou arisest for them.
Thou hast fashioned the earth according to thy desire,
thou alone, with men, cattle, and all wild beasts,
all that is upon the earth and goeth upon feet,
and all that soareth above and flieth with its wings.
Thou puttest every man in his place and thou suppliest
         [their needs . . .
Thou arisest in thy forms as living sun.
Thou makest millions of forms of thyself alone.
Thou thyself art lifetime and men live in thee.
The eyes look on thy beauty until thou settest.
Thou art in mine heart,
and there is none other that knoweth thee save thy son,
whom thou makest to comprehend thy designs and thy might,
the king of Upper and Lower Egypt,
who liveth on Truth,
lord of the Two Lands, the sole one of Rē,
son of Rē, who liveth on Truth,
lord of diadems, Ikhenaton, great in his duration.' 24

Among the people the new doctrine of Aton did not gain a firm hold.
The short epoch during which the heretical king of Amarna held
power passed without leaving any permanent traces. Akhnaton's successors reverted to the ancient national god Amun. The residence and
temple at Amarna fell into decay. The name of Akhnaton was erased
from memorials in order to obliterate his memory for all time.
During the subsequent Ramessid period men's religious attitudes
appear to have acquired a deeper spiritual content.
In the books of wisdom and funerary formulae one can detect a note
of sincere and ardent piety. In the Wisdom of Anii the following lines
occur:

'The dwelling of God,
it abhorreth clamour.
Pray with a loving heart,
all the words whereof are hidden.
Then he will do what thou needest;
he will hear what thou sayest
and accept thine offering.' 25

# X. ART AND ARCHITECTURE UNDER
# THE XVIIIth DYNASTY

ARCHI-
TECTURE
Shortly after the foundation of the New Kingdom its rulers sought
to demonstrate their power by embarking upon an ambitious programme of building. Not only royal and private tombs were constructed, but temples as well. The latter played a more important role than
they had before. In particular, a spacious and dignified place of worship had to be built near the capital for Amun, which would be fitting
for him in his position as the national god. The history of the construction of the gigantic temples at Karnak extends from the Middle Kingdom to the Ptolemaic era.

*Temples
at Karnak*

Fig. 37
An examination of the part played by the kings of the XVIIIth
Dynasty in developing this gigantic complex of buildings furnishes
ample information with regard to the evolution of architectural style
during the New Kingdom.

An alabaster chapel was erected by Amenophis I to contain 'the
barque of Amun'. Then Thutmosis I added the fourth and fifth
pylons and the two tall obelisks. The two pylons were massive gateways, built in a manner typical of the ensuing period. There were
flag-poles in front of them, and between them was a hall, in which
stood colossal statues of the king, manifest as the god Osiris, in niches
along the longitudinal walls. This hall was further embellished by
Thutmosis I's daughter, Hatshepsut, with two huge obelisks of red
Aswan granite.

She also built a pylon between the national temple and an older
shrine to the south, dedicated to the vulture goddess Mut, and thereby
established a relationship between these two sanctuaries. The colossi
of Amenophis I and Thutmosis I that stood in front of the pylon must
have been an impressive and majestic sight. Thutmosis III, the greatest military leader among the pharaohs of the XVIIIth Dynasty,
added two large halls, the so-called 'Halls of Annals'. On the walls
he recorded the campaigns he had undertaken and listed the booty
he had dedicated to the god Amun. The ceiling of the first hall was
supported by two granite pillars. On one of them is a bold relief of
papyri, the heraldic plant of Lower Egypt, and on the other a relief
of lilies, the Upper Egyptian symbol.

The only other source of information about the monuments added

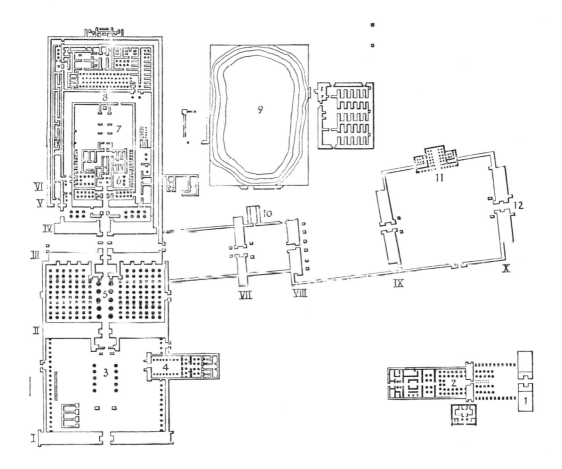

FIG. 37 — *Ground-plan of the national temple dedicated to the god Amun at Karnak.*
*Pylons I-X Cf. pp. 152, 215.*

1. *Ptolemy Euergetes Gate*
2. *Khons Temple*
3. *Amun Temple, Bubastide Hall contain-*
   *ing columns of Taharka*
4. *Ramses III Temple*
5. *Hypostyle Hall of Ramses II*
6. *Monuments of the XVIIIth Dynasty*
   *and Holy of Holies*

7. *Architectural ruins from the Middle*
   *Kingdom*
8. *Festival Hall of Thutmosis III*
9. *Sacred lake*
10. *Chapel of Thutmosis III*
11. *Temple of Amenophis II*
12. *Path to Temple of Mut*

153

FIG. 38    by Thutmosis III is the Festival Hall which this king built to the east of the complex that dates from Middle Kingdom times. This hall consists of three aisles of equal height, each subdivided by ten columns resembling tent-poles. Each aisle has a lower aisle, situated on the outside, with pillars running along it. In the upper part of the wall of the central aisle there are some clerestory windows. The hall must be regarded as the translation into stone of a festive tent. The three aisles give this basilica a simple elegance and harmonious symmetry that make it one of the most impressive examples of early New Kingdom art. Already during the reign of Thutmosis III columns in the form of plants replaced the strictly inorganic pillars which we find at the beginning of each of the great divisions of Egyptian history: in the Chephren Temple (Old Kingdom), the Mentuhotep Temple (Middle Kingdom), and now at the beginning of the New Kingdom as well.

In the temple at Karnak the rooms adjoining the Halls of Annals and the Festival Hall contain 16-sided papyrus-bundle columns, which serve to support the ceiling. One of the chapels built by Thutmosis III in the temple at Luxor has similar columns, with 8 shafts. From the reign of Amenophis II onwards pillars are finally superseded by columns in the form of plants.

*Temple at Luxor*    The temple at Luxor just mentioned, of which the greater part was built under Amenophis III, is dedicated to the triad of Amun, Mut

FIG. 39    and the moon-god Khons. Owing to the relatively good state of preservation we can gain an idea of temple architecture during the flowering period of the New Kingdom. The temple of Luxor was joined to the temple of Karnak by a paved avenue flanked by ram-headed sphinges, the sacred animal of Amun. Every year in a magnificent procession the idol of Amun was taken in the sacred barque up the Nile from Karnak to Luxor, where the marriage between the god and the goddess was celebrated. On entering the temple of Amenophis III we are confronted by a colonnade with seven papyriform columns on either side. They have elegantly curved capitals in the shape of open papyrus umbels. The adjoining court is surrounded on three sides by two rows of papyrus-bundle columns. This leads to the large columned hall, where the closely-packed papyriform columns and subdued light served to remind participants in the procession of the mysterious and solemn purpose of their festivities, and to put them into a proper state of awesome respect for the statues of the gods in the adjoining chapels. The style of the flowering period of the New Kingdom is characterized by soft and graceful lines and curves and a harmonious symmetry between the various elements. From the closing phase of the XVIIIth Dynasty, the Amarna Period, little has unfortunately survived. The monuments of Amenophis IV at Thebes were pulled down by Horemheb and the stones used by him to build pylons.

The temple which Amenophis IV erected at Amarna in honour of the new god was built in haste of mud-brick, and was doubtless destroyed shortly after the death of the heretical king. Its ground-plan can in part be traced. It consisted of a sequence of open courts, in which offerings were made to Aton on an altar in the open air.

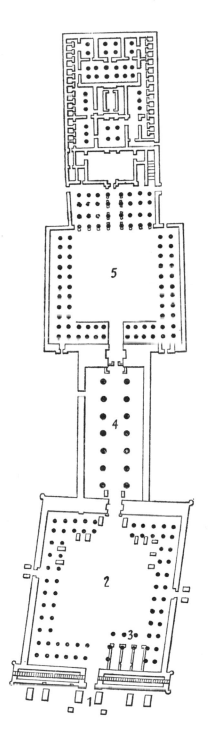

FIG. 39 — *Ground-plan of the temple at Luxor dedicated to the gods Amun, Mut and Khons. Cf. pp. 154, 189.*
1. *Pylon with statues and obelisks of Ramses II*
2. *Court of Ramses II*
3. *Columns of Thutmosis III*
4. *Colonnade of Amenophis III*
5. *Temple of Amenophis III*

The royal palace at Amarna comprised halls for official receptions and administrative purposes, of which only fragments of the painted stucco floor have been preserved. A corridor connected the official palace with the king's private residence. The latter contained apartments and other domestic quarters arranged around a garden. Outside the town was a pleasure-palace with gardens and artificial lakes, and in the north another palace where the architecture and paintings deserve special attention. The palace area was entered by way of two courts, situated one behind the other; one then came to the two columned halls, the Throne Room, and the smaller residential and reception rooms. To the north of the courts was a temple court, containing the altar and stables for animals. In the north-eastern part was a garden surrounded by a colonnade. Smaller rooms along the longitudinal sides presumably served to house poultry. From the large columned hall two corridors led to a staircase from which one could gain access to a small balcony.

A characteristic feature of the Amarna period is the importance attached to harmonious blending of the architecture with the natural setting. The layout is determined with an eye to aesthetic effect. Not only the walls, but also the floors, ceilings and columns bear paintings, the themes of which are drawn from nature.

In the layout of royal tombs there was an important change at the beginning of the New Kingdom. Amenophis I made a division between the cult temple and the tomb itself, in order to protect the costly treasures contained in the royal sarcophagus-chamber from thieves. Thutmosis I and his successors had their tombs built in a rocky defile in the mountains near Thebes, now known as the Valley of the Kings.

Fig. 40 The mortuary temples belonging to these tombs are situated on the edge of the fertile strip of land. Since it was intended to keep the existence of these tombs secret, none of the architecture is visible above ground. The tomb served merely to house the sarcophagus and funerary furnishings; the cult was performed in the valley-temple. The disposition of rooms in the royal tombs varies. Leading into the rock face is a winding corridor, or one with many right-angled turns, which eventually broadens out into a number of chambers or pillared halls, some larger than others, the walls of which are mostly embellished with scenes of a religious character.

Among the mortuary temples dating from the XVIIIth Dynasty we have the terraced temple of Queen Hatshepsut, which was built very close to the tomb of Mentuhotep II. Formerly a broad avenue flanked

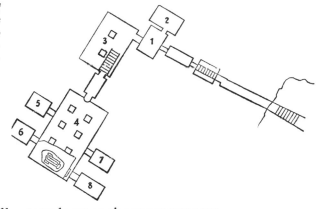

FIG. 40 — *Ground-plan of the tomb of Amenophis II, in the Valley of the Kings at Thebes. XVIIIth Dynasty, 1437-1410 B.C. 1. Shaft. 2. Ancillary chamber. 3. Vestibule. 4. Sarcophagus-chamber. 5-8. Ancillary chambers. Cf. p. 156.*

by sphinges led from the royal valley temple up to the mortuary temple. The latter was surrounded by gardens, trees and a massive enclosure wall. From the gateway a ramp led to the first terrace, on which stood two colonnades — one on the left and one on the right. The second terrace has the same plan, with two colonnades and side-chapels dedicated to Hathor, who was worshipped as goddess of the dead, and Anubis. Another ramp leads through a granite gateway to the uppermost terrace, and brings one into a court with two rows of columns running right round it. On the right-hand side is a portico, leading to another open court. This contained the altar used in the cult of the sun-god Rēhorakhty. On the left-hand side is the barrel-vaulted funerary chapel of the queen. The rear wall of the court is formed by the natural rock, into which chapels of varying size have been hewn. The material used in this building is almost exclusively limestone. Its gleaming light colour stands out against the yellowish-brown rock. The building has a simple elegance that enables it to blend well with the magnificent landscape. The ceilings are almost invariably supported by austere square or hexagonal pillars. The rocky setting, the temple, and the temple garden together form a harmonious whole. The mortuary temple of Hatshepsut no doubt incorporated ideas drawn from the Middle Kingdom terraced temple situated nearby. Similarly, the small temples with a gallery of pillars, that were so popular in the early XVIIIth Dynasty, also followed the tradition developed during the Middle Kingdom. The jubilee temple of Hatshepsut at Medinet Habu, which was later rebuilt by Thutmosis I, had a forerunner in Sesostris I's jubilee chapel at Karnak. A large number of private tombs from the XVIIIth Dynasty have survived. They are situated on the spurs of hilly ground that run

FIG. 41

down to the west bank of the river near Thebes. They consist of an entrance hall, at the far side of which is a gateway giving access to the sepulchral chambers, which are cut into the rock. First one passes through a hall sited at an oblique angle, and then a long narrow hall, before one finds oneself in the small chapel where the statue of the deceased stands. In the chapel and the forecourt are two shafts giving access to the sarcophagus-chamber, which is situated at a lower level. This layout was often varied. During the flowering period of the New Kingdom the sepulchral chambers are divided by columns and pillars. The size of the chambers and the splendour of the architecture are eloquent testimony to the wealth and power of the court officials. The tombs of Akhnaton's courtiers were built in the rocky mountains that rise to the east of the plain at Amarna. They have halls which, instead of being placed at an oblique angle, as in the Theban tombs, are usually almost square in plan, with columns in the shape of plants. Adjoining this hall is a simple transverse hall, which leads

into the small chapel with the statue. Many tombs remained unfinished, for after Akhnaton died and his successors returned to Thebes nobles and officials were once again buried in the city of the dead on the western bank of the river.

The spirit of the Pyramid Period is expressed most clearly in the monumental rigidity and clear definition of its architecture, that of the Middle Kingdom in its sculpture, and that of the New Kingdom in its paintings. These depict in a most convincing manner life as it was lived at the time.

Despite the Hyksos domination between the Middle and New Kingdoms, Thebes retained an artistic tradition that led to the production of many fine works.

In reliefs and paintings dating from the early XVIIIth Dynasty there is a tendency towards concentration and simplification in building up scenes, which shows that an attempt was being made at this time to

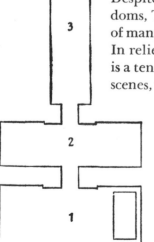

FIG. 41 — *Ground-plan of the complex of private tombs at Thebes. XVIIIth Dynasty, 1557-1304 B.C. 1. Forecourt. 2. Transverse hall. 3. Long hall. 4. Chapel. Cf. p. 157.*

PLATE 47 — King Tutankhamun wearing his royal head-dress: alabaster lid of a canopic jar. On the fore-head are the vulture's head and uraeus snake, the heraldic symbols of Upper and Lower Egypt. From the tomb of King Tutankhamun in the Valley of the Kings at Thebes. At burial the viscera of the deceased were interred in four canopic jars. New Kingdom, XVIIth Dynasty, approx. 1340 B.C. *Egyptian Museum, Cairo. Height 24 cm. Cf. p. 207.*

PLATE 48 — Pectoral bearing the name of Ramses II. From a mummy of Apis, found at Sakkara. Gold with cornelian, turquoise and lapis lazuli. New Kingdom, XIXth Dynasty, 1290-1224 B.C. *Louvre, Paris. Height 13 cm. Cf. p. 208*.

PLATE 49 — Gold vessel. From Bubastis. New Kingdom, XIXth Dynasty, approx. 1250 B.C. *Egyptian Museum, Cairo, Height 11.5 cm. Cf. p. 208.*

PLATE 50 — Wooden unguent-spoon in the shape of a girl swimming and reaching out to touch a duck. From Abu Gurob in the Faiyum. New Kingdom, XVIIIth Dynasty, approx. 1370 B.C. *Egyptian Museum, Cairo. Length 30 cm. Cf. p. 208.*

FIG. 42 — *The ram-headed God of Creation, Khnum, forming the body of Queen Hatshepsut and her ka. The ka is the immortal substance of man which corresponds roughly to our word 'soul'. Detail of limestone relief in the Mortuary Temple of Hatshepsut at Deir el-Bahari, Thebes. XVIIIth Dynasty, 1490-approx. 1470 B.C. Cf. p. 60; below.*

reach a new definition of artistic style.

The best examples of the style adopted for Thutmosid reliefs are the sequences of lavish scenes in the Mortuary Temple of Queen Hatshepsut. Their light and delicate colours evoke a mood of gaiety and *joie de vivre.* 26

*Reliefs on royal monuments*

The lower hall, situated to the north, contains fragments of a scene showing birds being trapped by means of a clap-net. In the southern hall is a detailed composition representing the erection of the two obelisks presented by the queen to the temple at Karnak. On the northern side of the central terrace is the important scene of the conception and birth of the queen, and on the southern side is a series of scenes depicting in detail the expedition to Punt, the land of incense. Punt is portrayed with almost scientific exactitude: it has beehive-shaped huts, various plants and trees, and a princess who is charmingly characterized — with a lined face and a corpulent body. The keen sense of observation and the loving attention to detail give the impression of a lively reportage.

This delight in the accurate recording of actual events is also evident in the reliefs carved in a room of the festive temple of Thutmosis III at Karnak. This room is called 'the Botanical Gardens' on account of the naturalistic treatment of the animals and plants brought back by

FIG. 42

FIG. 43

163

Fig. 43 — *Native huts in the Punt. Detail of lime-stone reliefs in the Mortuary Temple of Queen Hatshepsut at Deir el-Bahari, Thebes. XVIIIth Dynasty, 1490 - approx. 1470 B.C. Cf. p. 163.*

the king from his Syrian campaign. In the low reliefs, executed with a fine sense of modelling, accurate reportage is combined with a joy-ous delight in natural phenomena. Thutmosis III's summary lists of military events and pictures of booty in the Hall of Annals at Karnak are the products of a sense of history and a desire to record events with the utmost accuracy for the benefit of posterity.

*‹Reliefs and paint-ings in private tombs at Thebes* Whereas the decorations on the walls in the royal monuments are reliefs, executed in the traditional manner, in the tombs of private persons at Thebes painting comes into its own. One reason for this may be that the limestone here was too brittle for reliefs; artistic considerations must also have played some part as well. The walls were at first coated with a mixture of clay and chaff, and then plaster-ed with white stucco.

The range of subjects is further enlarged during the XVIIIth Dyn-asty. Pictures showing new techniques, such as chariot-building, are added to the repertoire. Religious scenes are enriched by detailed descriptions of ritual acts and ceremonies performed at the burial of the deceased. Ceilings are painted with ornamental designs.

FIG. 44 In pictures showing the deeds of the lord of the tomb during his tenure of office we cannot help but be struck by the evidence of the vast expanse of the Egyptian empire. Foreign embassies presenting gifts, tributary foreigners, and files of prisoners remind us that men's experiences were no longer confined to events that transpired within the country's borders. From the Thutmosid era onwards the king is also portrayed on the walls of tombs — usually enthroned beneath a canopy, being worshipped by the dead. This is of assistance in estab-lishing the deceased's life-span.

Pictures bearing on earthly life embellish the transverse hall, while religious scenes are to be found in the long hall and the adjoining chapel. Along the shorter sides of the transverse hall are two stelae. One served as a place of worship, instead of the false door of Old

Kingdom times. The other was a memorial to the deceased, which told the story of his life.

The hunting scenes now sometimes feature horses and chariots, which FIG. 45 were not known prior to the Hyksos period. The landscape is shown as hilly desert country. The animals hunted are represented either in headlong flight or facing the hunter in a threatening manner. The scene has a dramatic sense of movement which conveys something of the excitement of the chase. The ancient motif of the feast of the dead obtains a new meaning. It now depicts the annual festival arranged by the living for the 'Feast of the Valley'. For this festival Amun crosses to the western bank of the Nile in his barque to visit the goddess Hathor in her temple at Deir el-Bahari. The procession to escort the image of the god is followed in the evening by banquets, with music and dancing in the tombs of the deceased.

During the early XVIIIth Dynasty scenes are composed of loosely arranged figures with clearly-defined outlines. Gestures are used to suggest states of mind. Together with the astringent charm of the graceful forms and movements, they reflect the aristocratic reticence and dignity of the courtly world.

During the reigns of Thutmosis IV and Amenophis III a new style can be detected in reliefs and paintings. The large number of them that have survived from this period include some of the finest works that Egypt ever produced.

AGE OF
MATURITY

Not very many of them are reliefs in temples. In the temple at Luxor Amenophis III had replicas made in relief of the divine birth of the king, represented in the same manner as in the Mortuary Temple of Hatshepsut. They are executed in a fine and elegant style. In most cases mural reliefs keep to the old tradition: there are numerous sequences depicting the king in company with the gods.

*Reliefs in temples*

The battles and campaigns that were apparently once represented on pylons and temple walls have not survived. These must have been magnificent works, both from the standpoint of composition and the attention given to detail. Some idea of their splendour can be gained

FIG. 44 — *Syrian princes bearing tribute. Mural from the tomb of Sebekhotep at Thebes. XVIIIth Dynasty, approx. 1400 B.C. British Museum. Width 1.29 m. Cf. pp. 164, 166.*

FIG. 45 — *Hunting in the desert. Relief in the tomb of Rekhmara at Thebes. XVIIIth Dynasty, approx. 1500-1450 B.C. Cf. p. 165.*

FIG. 46 from the scenes showing one of Thutmosis IV's chariots. From the Archaic Period onwards the pharaoh was depicted in symbolic form triumphing over his vanquished enemies, seizing them by a tuft of hair as they sink to the ground before him, and despatching them with a club. This motif already occurs on the Narmer palette. It soon became a standard formula to denote a victorious ruler. But in the scene with the chariot the king is shown taking a leading part in the fray.

An impression of the drama and movement of battle is evoked by the unnatural position of the various figures, which frequently overlap one another. The accuracy with which the Syrian enemies are portrayed, by emphasizing differences of costume and racial features, suggests that this is a representation of an actual event. The extent to which this animated scene departs from the traditional mode is illustrated by the fact that some of the Asiatic warriors who have been thrown to the ground are depicted with their heads *en face,* turned towards the viewer, thus infringing the law whereby figures are shown either in direct full-face or in direct profile.

Whereas temple art is restricted to specific motifs, represented in a traditional manner, the murals in private tombs display a wealth of motifs and modes of expression which convey an excellent idea of the attitude of mind of men living in this, the most magnificent epoch of Egyptian art.

*Reliefs and paintings in private tombs at Thebes*

Instead of the harsh austerity of form and the accurate arrangement of figures characteristic of the early XVIIIth Dynasty, we have a soft engaging style, which occasionally evokes the mood of the scene One mural in the tomb of Sebekhotep, dating from the reign of Thutmosis IV, shows an embassy of Syrian princes bringing tribute. They

FIG. 44 are distinguished from Egyptians by their garments, beards and coiffures, and are depicted striding along at the rear of the group, in the traditional posture of men making offerings. But the three figures in front are on bended knee, a posture indicating their subjection to the power of the Egyptian pharaoh. Two of them are shown with their arms raised; one of them has cast himself to the ground and is touching it with his forehead. These gestures still have an element of symbolism. They generalize a situation that doubtless occurred frequently in those days. The effect produced is similar to that of an illustration to a phrase that often appears in Egyptian texts: '... and there they lay flat on their faces before his majesty ...'

A composition showing birds being hunted with wooden throw-sticks PLATE P. 91 in a thicket of papyrus exemplifies the picturesque beauty and gentle flowing elegance of line that artists were capable of attaining. It originates from a tomb at Thebes built during the flowering period of the New Kingdom. Papyrus reeds, birds and fish are shown with subtle shadings of colour. The kilt worn by the lord of the tomb, the garment worn by his wife, their wigs and jewellery are all worked

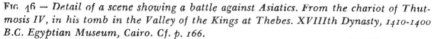

FIG. 46 — *Detail of a scene showing a battle against Asiatics. From the chariot of Thutmosis IV, in his tomb in the Valley of the Kings at Thebes. XVIIIth Dynasty, 1410-1400 B.C. Egyptian Museum, Cairo. Cf. p. 166.*

FIG. 47 — *Detail of banqueting scene showing female musicians and dancing-girls. Mural from the tomb of Neb-Amun at Thebes. XVIIIth Dynasty, approx. 1400 B.C. British Museum. Cf below*

with meticulous care. The pictorial effect derives from the fact that it is conceived as a painting. The gentle curves are exquisitely drawn.

PLATE P. 92 Banqueting scenes offered an especially tempting opportunity to depict all the splendour of convivial court society. Beneath the festive robes the curves of the body can be made out; the jewellery is lavish and the wigs dainty; on the women's garments there are even stains of oil spilt from the ointment-cones which they are carrying on their

PLATE P. 93 heads. All these details show that the artists approached their subjects as painters. The tender beauty of the women, the comely bodies of the young maidens, and the graceful movements of the dancers and musicians are expressed in soft sensitive flowing lines and a delicate range of colours.

Tension and harmony are produced by grouping the figures together in the performance of a common action, and by depicting gestures and expressions suggestive of a common spiritual experience. There is a tendency towards novel and unusual pictorial effects, attained by means of overlapping and foreshortening. The result is a picture that is close to nature, as may be seen from a wall-painting from the

FIG. 47 tomb of Neb-Amum, which shows graceful nude female dancers and musicians — the latter viewed frontally, with their heads inclined to one side.

FIG. 48 Lamenting women, who are an important element in burial scenes, lend themselves particularly to the expression of intense emotion. Their gestures suggest deep uncontrollable sorrow.

AMARNA PERIOD 1362-1304 B.C. Towards the end of the XVIIIth Dynasty, with the development of

168

Amarna art, the last step is taken towards a sensitive, refined and spiritual mode of expression. Together with the quest for a true god in religion there goes an endeavour to represent human beings in a manner true to life. The fanaticism of the reformer leads to overstated and exaggerated forms. The emphasis is on monotheism, on the person of the king as ruler and sole prophet of the new god Aton. In addition to the motif of the royal couple standing below a radiant Aton, which occurs frequently, there are family scenes of an intimate character. Such themes as the rewarding of meritorious courtiers or the granting of audience to foreign envoys offer artists the chance to illustrate, in an expressive vibrating interplay of lines, their inner experience of a hypersensitive moribund world.

The reliefs in the tomb of the vizier Ramose possess a solemn dignified beauty. They date from the transitional period between the reign of Amenophis III and that of his son Amenophis IV (Akhnaton). There are two images of Amenophis IV in Ramose's tomb. 27 In a relief which was begun when he came to the throne, he and the goddess Maat are shown under a canopy receiving the veneration of the lord of the tomb. Subject and style are in complete conformity with those customary in the flowering period of the New Kingdom. The second composition, in which Amenophis IV (Akhnaton) appears with his consort Nefertiti, over the ledge of a window under a radiant Aton, may be ascribed to the fourth year of the king's reign. It shows distinctly the sudden emergence of an expressive new style in lieu of that current in the reign of Amenophis III — a gentle style with delicate lines.

In the rock-tombs belonging to court officials from Amarna the royal family is represented far more frequently than subjects relating to

*Reliefs in private tombs at Thebes*

PLATE P. 94

FIG. 48  *Wailing women Detail of a mural showing the funeral of Ramose, in his tomb at Thebes. XVIIIth Dynasty, approx. 1360 B.C. Cf. p. 168.*

FIG. 49

the life of the deceased in this world or the beyond. Pride of place is taken by the composition showing the royal family under the radiant Aton, which (leaving out of consideration its artistic merits) is an impressive memorial to the new doctrine and its 'sole prophet'. The king is depicted in a most realistic manner: pot-bellied, with stout thighs but spindly legs and arms. An excessively long thin neck supports a narrow head; the face is flabby, with an elongated chin and thick lips. The accentuated ugliness of his figure is offset by the deep spirituality evident in his gestures and expression. Towards the close of the Amarna period all exaggeration is discarded and the style again becomes more moderate and relaxed. The intimate private life of the royal family serves as the theme of sensitive genre scenes with an abundance of gestures, which convey something of the charm inherent in deep personal experience. It is not the subject that makes

FIG. 49 — *King Amenophis IV( Akhnaton) and his family making sacrificial offerings to Aton. Limestone relief from the tomb of a princess at Amarna. According to the Aton cult, introduced by Amenophis IV (Akhnaton), the sun in the heavens is a great goddess, the creator and preserver of all life. The rays of the sun terminate in hands holding the symbol for 'life'. XVIIIth Dynasty, 1363-1346 B.C. Egyptian Museum, Cairo. Height 52 cm. Cf. above .*

FIG. 50 — *Foreign ambassadors. Detail of a limestone relief from the tomb of King Horemheb (as he later became), near Memphis. XVIIIth Dynasty, approx. 1330 B.C. Rijksmuseum van Oudheden, Leyden. Cf. below*

these pictures so impressive, but rather the mood that emanates from them. In lieu of exaggerated ugliness, there is an engaging elegance and a poetic mood best illustrated in the composition known as 'the Promenade in the Garden'. PLATE P. 111

Among the treasures found in the tomb of Tutankhamun, son-in-law of Akhnaton, are works of dazzling beauty which combine the enhanced depth of feeling and expressiveness of movement found PLATE P. 112 in Amarna style with the elegant and gentle style of the reign of Amenophis III.

Echoes of Amarna art are also apparent in reliefs from the tombs *Echoes of Amarna style* of General Horemheb and the High Priest Neferronpet in Lower Egypt. Those in the Horemheb tomb reflect the spirituality of the Amarna period. It is evident in the grouping of figures in move- FIG. 50 ment and the penetrating, psychologically acute interpretation of the events depicted.

The scene showing a funeral procession in the Neferronpet tomb FIG. 51 suggests, in the mourning figures, the spiritual frame of mind of those participating in the ceremony.

The wall decorations in the tombs were worked in relief — in most *Paintings in the palaces at Amarna* cases in sunk relief — but those in the palaces and dwelling-houses at Amarna were painted.

The new possibilities open to painters are manifest in the delicate nuances of colour and bold overlappings in the picture of Akhnaton's PLATE P. 113 two daughters, from his urban palace at Amarna. The two princesses are shown naked, bedecked with jewels, and with delicately modelled limbs, squatting upon leather cushions. The contour lines of the bodies, the chin, cheeks and heels are painted in a darker shade. This makes for a plastic and animated effect.

In the Amarna palaces the floors were painted as well. Colourful landscapes show ponds full of fish, and jungle scenes with birds and various kinds of plants. Almost invariably they were painted without any preliminary drawing or outline being made. The line plays hardly any role at all; the laws of composition are no longer observed, and instead the colours merge gradually into one another. The unrestrained artistic licence of the paintings expresses a genuine feeling for nature that at times even amounts to enthusiasm. Nature is now accounted worthy of representation for its own sake, instead of merely providing a framework for some particular event to be depicted. In the Amarna period nature — peaceful, yet abounding in vitality — makes a direct appeal to one's senses.

In the 'Green Room' of the pleasure-palace at Amarna the wall-paintings are not broken at the corners; instead the room is conceived as a single unit. The portrayal of nature does not call for division of the scene so much as for creation of a general atmosphere, one inviting calm contemplation.

The pharaohs of the XVIIIth Dynasty ruled for approximately 200 years. During this period Egypt undertook great wars of conquest, enjoyed glory as a major world power, and also experienced the first signs of decline — in the spiritual and religious foundations of the state, as well as politically. The artistic achievements of the period reflect the transformations that took place in men's approach to life. Out of the austerity and precision of the two-dimensional style that prevailed at the beginning of the New Kingdom there develops the soft fluidity and elegant draughtsmanship of the golden age. This is followed by Amarna art, the exaggerated expression of a spiritualized and slightly decadent world which, in the light of the traditions of Egyptian art, come close to disintegration. Towards the end of the XVIIIth Dynasty there emerges a more harmonious balanced style that penetrates into the depths of man's spiritual experience.

FIG. 51 — Mourners. Detail of a limestone relief showing a funeral procession. From the tomb of the High Priest Neferronpet at Memphis. New Kingdom, XVIIIth Dynasty, approx. 1330 B.C. Berlin. Cf. p. 171.

Like the Middle Kingdom, the New Kingdom began after a period of political chaos in which artistic activity almost ceased. In both cases it was possible for a new style to develop at Thebes in Upper Egypt, which was only to a slight extent affected by the unrest. Architects, painters and sculptors were favoured by the fact that the royal residence and the seat of government were both at Thebes. They faced major tasks, and it was in the process of solving them that they were able to evolve the new style. At first men were highly conscious of the great achievements that Egyptian art had to its credit, and made a deliberate effort to return to the artistic traditions of the past. Thus at the beginning of the New Kingdom one may plainly detect the influence of Upper Egyptian art in early Middle Kingdom times. The well-balanced austerity of the works dating from the reign of Sesostris I suited the climate of the early New Kingdom. This attitude of mind provided the basis on which Thutmosid art developed an individual style that sprang from men's experience of the times in which they lived.

The works of the XVIIth Dynasty still manifest a certain hardness and lack of assurance in the treatment of form, which they lose by the beginning of the XVIIIth Dynasty.

A large number of statues in the round have survived from the reign of Queen Hatshepsut. They were discovered in a quarry to which they were banished by Thutmosis III after her death, so that her memory might cease to haunt him. They include images of Hatshepsut in a seated, striding or kneeling posture, and also a group of sphinges. Almost all of them depict her as a man, with the attributes of royal power. The stylistic affinities between some of these statues and others from the Middle Kingdom are unmistakable. But the frankness, charm and vitality of the faces suggest a new attitude to life. Since the figures were kept in a secret hiding-place, the painting on them has been preserved sufficiently well for it to be ascertained that limestone or sandstone statues were painted all over, whereas in the case of those of hard stone only individual parts, such as eyes, jewellery, hair and inscriptions were coloured.

There are also a large number of statues in the round of Thutmosis III, showing the pharaoh as a taut figure of youthful buoyancy, with wide-awake eyes. The image of the royal commander has greater vitality and rigidity than was the case with Old Kingdom royal statues, in which emphasis was laid upon the exalted divine nature of the ruler, and at the same time has more determination and immediacy

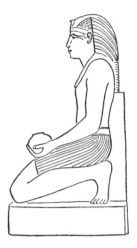

FIG. 52 — *King Thutmosis III making a sacrificial offering. Figure of white marble. From Deir el-Medina, Thebes. XVIIIth Dynasty, approx. 1470-1437 B.C. Egyptian Museum, Cairo. Height 38.7 cm. Cf. below*

FIG. 52

than the serious meditative royal statues from the Middle Kingdom. Standing and seated figures are shown in a posture that conforms to the tradition of temple sculpture, but the statues of the king kneeling, in the act of offering water or wine to the gods, have a noble restrained expression and a graceful vital silhouette.

The royal statues were at one time erected in temples where they could be seen. In the New Kingdom their purpose was not only to serve as a memorial to the ruler, but to produce an aesthetic impression upon the viewer.

In the statuary produced during the reigns of Amenophis II and Thutmosis IV the style becomes looser and more refined. The tense vitality of the early XVIIIth Dynasty gives way by the time of Amenophis II to a suave and charming manner that suggests the spirit within.

With a group of statues showing Thutmosis IV and his mother the figure of the pharaoh descends from the lonely peak of absolute power to the world of family life. [28] The crude portliness is evidence of the trend towards realism, and is far removed from the youthful and austere idealized portrait of the ruler favoured at the beginning of the New Kingdom.

*Figures of private persons*

PLATE P. 114

Figures of private persons carved at this time copy the style of royal statues. Court officials, military commanders and priests are usually shown life-size, in conformity with their new enhanced importance. As had already been the case during the Middle Kingdom, the king gave senior officials the privilege of having statues of themselves erected in the temple. These temple statues were generally carved in the form of a block-statue or a 'Naos-bearer', a priest carrying a shrine with an idol. The inscriptions on the statues now contain, not only a request to the spectator to participate in the ritual and to say a prayer for the deceased, but also a detailed account of the latter's life on earth. This is proof of the new self-awareness that had evolved at this time in the upper strata of society.

Among the block-statues particular importance attaches to the figure of Senmut, tutor to Queen Hatshepsut's younger daughter. Only the head projects from the cube formed by the cloak wrapped around the squatting figure. The shape of the block-statue is taken from the Middle Kingdom, as is also the rather reserved, serious and dignified expression. Furthermore, it was in this era that these cloaked figures were evolved to represent official personages.

PLATE P. 131

In contrast to royal sculpture, the statues of dignitaries at the Theban court have a prosaic, reserved and aristocratic character.

The golden age of the New Kingdom begins with the statues of Amenophis III. These continue the trend towards a natural and human portrait that was evident in the statues of Thutmosis IV and his mother.

ACE OF
MATURITY

The gentle rounded volumes of the body, elegantly curved lines, and careful modelling of the fine drapery of the robes, the costly wigs and jewellery — all these features express the pretentious courtly culture of the day, which attached great value to external splendour. As well as official statues of Amenophis III, which follow the traditional manner of representation and evoke a sense of pathos and

*Royal sculpture*

FIG. 53 — *King Amenophis III. Brownish slate. XVIIIth Dynasty, 1400 1362 B.C. Metropolitan Museum, New York. Height 22 cm. Cf. p. 176.*

shallowness, there have survived figures of smaller dimensions, in which the pharaoh is portrayed in a more naturalistic manner. A slate statuette, now in New York, depicts the ruler as a rotund thickset figure. His hands are crossed, resting on his protruding abdomen. 29 This portliness and highly unroyal posture anticipates Amarna works. A tendency towards realism is also manifest in the ebony statuette of Amenophis III, now in the Brooklyn Museum. In the full face one can detect individualistic touches. The fine small ebony head of Tiy, the commoner who married Amenophis III, forms a transition to Amarna style. The statuettes of Amenophis III just mentioned make an attempt at realistic rendering of the individual person depicted. But the little head of Tiy does more: it embodies the profoundly spiritual turn of mind which this queen of humble origin possessed. The corners of her mouth are turned down, and there are deep grooves beside her nostrils. These traits evoke an impression of haughty disdain. The narrow slanting eyes have an icy and rather censorious stare.

With the attempt at psychological interpretation Egyptian art is set upon the road that in the short-lived Amarna epoch leads it to the limits of its formal laws.

The changes made in the carving of figures of private persons during the flowering period of the New Kingdom conform to those of royal sculpture. Amenophis, son of Hapu, one of the chief court dignitaries,

FIG. 53

PLATE P. 132

*Figures of private persons*

176

who was responsible for the colossi of Memnon in front of the Mortuary Temple of Amenophis III, now completely destroyed, obtained the right to put up several statues of himself in the temple at Karnak, and even to erect a mortuary temple of his own on the western bank of the river at Thebes. Among his temple statues one again finds the characteristic figure of the scribe. The alert vitality such figures possessed in the Old Kingdom now gives way to a suggestion of meditation and composure. The head is tilted slightly forwards; the gentle contours lack the intensity and precision they had had earlier. In another type of statue Amenophis, son of Hapu, is shown kneeling, FIG. 54 the posture of the legs concealed by his robe. The hands are shown resting on the thighs; the body is treated summarily; the face, with its sunken wrinkled features, is that of a wise old man absorbed in thought. As in the case of the small head of Queen Tiy, there is about it a sense of spirituality, of withdrawal from this kaleidoscopic and conflict-torn world, of the superiority that comes from a lofty critical mind.

The variety of the works that have survived shows that the men of the New Kingdom in its golden age had a number of ways open to them whereby they could express their attitude to life.

During this epoch developments took place which prepared the **AMARNA** ground for the spiritual convulsions of the Amarna era. Life at court **PERIOD** was characterized by prosperity and luxurious living which weakened men's moral fibre. The state religion had grown rigid to the point of shallow pathos. Festive rites celebrated in great splendour merely served to conceal its inner emptiness. Life had become richer and

*FIG. 55 — King Amenophis IV (Akhnaton). Head of the colossal sandstone statue from the temple at Karnak. XVIIIth Dynasty, approx. 1360 B.C. Total height originally approx. 4 m. Egyptian Museum, Cairo. Cf. p. 178.*

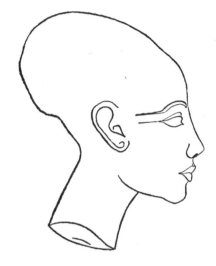

more varied — and also more complex and sensitive, so far as its spiritual foundations were concerned. It was no coincidence that a beginning was made at this time with the artistic representation of psychological and religious phenomena. The vital thread of human existence had been broken.

These were the conditions that the young king Amenophis IV found when he ascended the throne. With fanatical seriousness he embarked on a search for the deeper meaning of a life that had simultaneously become richer and emptier. He began with the quest for truth, of which there had been some evidence in the statuary of his father. However, his zeal for reform led him to break with the religious and artistic forms of the past, and to engage in exaggeration and overstatement, as a result of which the truthful content was once again lost. Amarna art at its best reflects the longing for a divine world — a world which had, however, already found expression in the timeless image of the god-king of the Pyramid Period: its unity between the terrestrial and supernatural planes of existence came much nearer to the ideal that Amenophis IV sought than the ecstatic exaggeration of effect of Amarna art, which attempted to confine within formal limitations something that could not be subjected to any form devised by human hands.

*Royal sculpture at Thebes*

In the pillared hall of the Aton Temple at Thebes, erected by Amenophis IV early in his reign, stood colossal statues of the king, made of painted sandstone. Parts of these have survived. The narrow face with the sagging chin, the full curving lips and slanting narrow eyes

FIG. 55

PLATE 51 — Bull of Apis. Detail of a painting on the wooden bottom-board of a coffin. Late Period, approx. 700 B.C. *Pelizaeus Museum, Hildesheim.* Cf. *pp. 214, 220.*

PLATE 52 — Ivory statuette of a member of the royal family.
Late Period, XXVth Dynasty, approx. 700 B.C. *Royal Scottish Museum, Edinburgh. Height 20 cm. Cf. p. 219.*

PLATE 53 — Queen Karomama, consort of Takeloth II. Bronze, inlaid with gold, silver, electrum and copper. ▶
Libyan Period, XXIInd Dynasty, 950-730 B.C. *Louvre, Paris. Height 59 cm. Cf. p. 209.*

PLATE 54 — Gold handle of a mirror belonging to King Shabaka, in the shape of a palmiform column around which are four deities in high relief. Late Period, approx. 700 B.C. *Museum of Fine Arts, Boston. Height 14.3 cm. Cf. p. 219.*

PLATE 55 — **Bronze statue of the god Osiris depicted in a close-fitting mummy-swathing with a collar necklace, holding a scourge and sceptre. On his head he wears a crown of horns and plumes with the uraeus snake. Below the chin is the beard that forms part of the ceremonial dress worn by royalty: it occurs only in representations of gods and kings. Late Period, 7th-6th cents. B.C.** *Kestner Museum, Hanover. Height 34.4 cm. Cf. p. 220.*

PLATE 56 — Bronze Horus falcon. Late Period, 7th-6th cents. B.C. *Walters Art Gallery, Baltimore. Height 22.5 cm. Cf. p. 220.*

convey the impression of intelligence, but also of fanatical enthusiasm. The points of exaggeration that occur are due to a desire to break with tradition and represent the new religious ideas in an impressive form. The body, with its bony clavicles, fleshy chest and bloated abdomen, is morbid in its deformity. The arms and the lower part of the legs are spindly. Instead of a harmonious blending of proportions there is a lack of balance and a distortion that suggests nervosity and decadence. Judged by the formal laws of Egyptian art, that of the Amarna period represents a major break from stylistic tradition. It may be explained in large part by the revolutionary and fanatical character of the heretical king.

Although the reliefs discovered at Amarna which represent the king below the radiant Aton are executed in the same style as the colossi at Thebes, the statues in the round from Amarna are devoid of all distortion or exaggeration. They may be compared rather with the suave and sensitive style associated with the reign of Amenophis III. Most of the works of sculpture from the Amarna period known to us are models from workshops and unfinished parts. The material used was either limestone, sandstone or most frequently plaster; granite was rarer. *Royal sculpture at Amarna*

PLATE P. 133

The models discovered in Amarna workshops include the well-known bust of Nefertiti, the royal consort of King Akhnaton. The delicate charm of the features suggests an enigmatic and reserved personality. The cryptic look, the fine curvature of the lips, the narrow face and noble features are characteristic of Late Amarna style as it was cultivated in the reign of Tutankhamun. PLATE P. 134

A separate group is made up of heads of princesses that are distinguished by the curious projection of the back of the head. This is presumably based upon some deformity that was hereditary in Akhnaton's family. The fact that the artists did not shrink from representing it, as they doubtless would have done in earlier days, indicates their concern to produce a true image — and possibly also to the delight they took in curved contour lines. The popularity of this sweeping curve at the back of the head was such that even court officials had themselves portrayed in this manner, although they were certainly not afflicted by the same physical deformity. FIG. 56

The plaster models of heads and masks discovered in Amarna workshops were made during the course of production. They give a great deal of valuable information about the technical process involved, and stylistic development, but of course cannot be compared with *Models of masks*

PLATE P. 135

finished works that were produced at this time, or earlier. The process was as follows: first of all a model in clay was made; individual parts (such as the ears, for instance) were made separately in a mould and then affixed; from the clay model, which consisted of several parts, a plaster mould was taken and filled in with plaster; finally the mould was broken and the plastic cast served the sculptor as the guide in his work.

We shall probably never be able to tell whether the clay masks were taken from living persons, as one might be inclined to think when looking at the various facial expressions and differently shaped heads. There can, in any case, be no doubt that during this preparatory stage the greatest attention was paid to the meticulous rendering of nature. At the same time, it should not be overlooked that already with the plaster masks there is a transformation of the real image, a stylization, which attempts to do justice to the true inner expression. This was the main concern of sculptors during the Amarna period.

After the death of Akhnaton and the subsequent iconoclasm, designed to obliterate the memory and name of the heretical king, his son-in-law Tutankhamun developed a style characterized by gentle harmony and animated beauty. This was the fruit of the ecstatic exaggerations of the Amarna period, which at the end of the XVIIIth Dynasty gave us works of perfect grace and symmetry.

*Sculpture of private persons*

Although statues of private persons recede wholly into the background during the Amarna period, from the reign of Tutankhamun we have statues in the round as well as group compositions. These show that Amarna style and the echoes it evoked represent a late stage in spiritual and artistic development — one in which a slight note of decadence can be detected.

# XI. ART AND ARCHITECTURE IN
# THE RAMESSID ERA

ARCHITEC-
TURE *Early
XIXth Dynasty*

*Temple at Karnak*

The manifold internal and external problems that faced General
(later King) Horemheb in his efforts to restore Egypt to her position
as a world power left him little time to construct buildings of a
representative character. During his reign the temple at Karnak was
enlarged by the addition of the 9th and 10th pylons. For this purpose
blocks were taken from the Aton Temple of Amenophis IV. As a
mortuary temple Horemheb took over the complex built by Eye on
the western bank of the river at Thebes, enlarged it, and built a palace
connected to it. After his successful campaign against the Nubians
he had a small chapel erected in the southern part of Upper Egypt,
not far from Gebel Silsila.

*Temple at Abydos*

FIG. 57

Under Seti I and his son Ramses II a very large number of buildings
came to be erected throughout the country. At Abydos there appeared, in addition to the mortuary chapel which Seti I built for his
father Ramses I, the main temple dedicated to the seven deities,
which was not completed until the reign of Ramses II. It has two
slightly sloping courts, situated one behind the other, at the rear
of which are two pillared porticos. From here two hypostyle halls,
also built on an incline, lead to the seven offering-chapels. The
papyrus-bundle columns in the two halls have cushion-like bases and
smooth bulging shafts; they resemble the natural prototype only in
their calyx-leaves, suggested by low relief. The shafts of the columns
are covered with figures and inscriptions, so that the plant motif is
completely lost from view. The columns themselves are massive and
clumsy. The dominating feature is their gigantic size, and there is
not, as in the XVIIIth Dynasty, an elegant interplay between the
various architectural elements.

FIG. 75

*Osireion*

In the environs of the temple Seti I built a tomb for himself, the
so-called Osireion, which was executed in a completely different style.
Neither figures nor inscriptions are featured on its smooth walls.
The massive rectilinear pillars recall the austerity of Pyramid Period
architecture, whereas the layout of the temple complex as a whole
follows the pattern of the Osiris Tomb at Abydos, which was a popular place of pilgrimage from the Middle Kingdom onwards. As is
evident from the representations and texts in the side-chambers, the
architectonic structure of the building was governed by the funerary
rites performed there for the king, who was deemed to have become

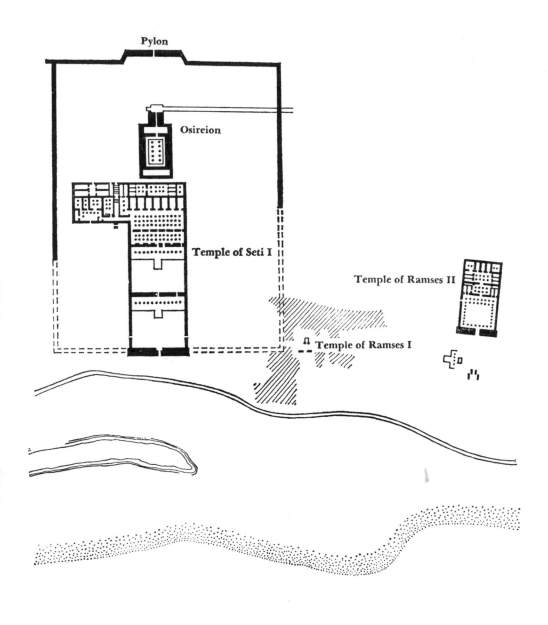

Pylon

Osireion

**Temple of Seti I**

Temple of Ramses II

Temple of Ramses I

Fig. 57 — *Ground-plan of temples of Ramses I, Seti I and Ramses II, and Osireion of Seti I, at Abydos. XIXth Dynasty. Cf. p. 187.*

an Osiris. The return to Old Kingdom forms gave it an austere and timeless character which to the owner, no doubt, seemed more appropriate than the evanescent style of the XIXth Dynasty. The burial-chamber of the Osireion remained empty; the mummy of Seti I was later interred in the Valley of the Kings.

The vast number of buildings put up by Ramses II in various parts of the country during the course of his long reign have made his name immortal. Until our own times it has been these monuments from the Ramessid era that have made the strongest impression upon visitors, for whom they are a symbol of ancient Egyptian culture as such. In addition to these new edifices he also altered or enlarged a considerable number of existing monuments. This work was not always executed with due sensitivity or care, so that the impressive quantity of buildings is not matched by a correspondingly high quality of workmanship; the latter is often rough and perfunctory. TEMPLES OF RAMSES II

One of the finest works of the early Ramessid period is the great Hypostyle Hall in the temple at Karnak, situated between the pylons built by Horemheb and Amenophis III. The 134 columns — of which those in the central aisle measure 21 metres and those in the side aisles 13 metres in height — give the impression of a vast forest of columns. Even today its superhuman grandeur makes a tremendous impact upon those who see it. It was once the setting for ritual processions and must have aroused in those who took part in them a feeling of awesome respect for the laws of eternity. *Karnak* FIG. 58

The temple at Luxor was also enlarged. Ramses II added to the north part of the complex a court containing statues and a huge pylon which, in its coarse workmanship, differs markedly from those parts of the temple built by Amenophis III, which have a symmetrical beauty. *Luxor* FIG. 39

The temple which the king erected at Abydos for the god Osiris and his own funerary rites has unfortunately been badly damaged. It is perhaps the most lavish monument built by Ramses II.

His actual mortuary temple, the so-called Ramesseum, lies on the western bank of the river at Thebes. The remains that have survived of the pylon, hypostyle hall and the massive Osiride pillars still evoke an impression of the monumental effect this magnificent building must have had upon contemporaries. Of the temples built by Ramses II in the province of Nubia special attention must be paid to the rock-cut temple at Abu Simbel, on the southern border. The mountains which jut forward to the bank of the river suggested the idea PLATE P. 137 *Abu Simbel* PLATE P. 138

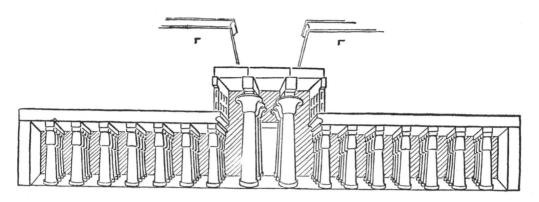

FIG. 58 — *Cross-section of the huge Hypostyle Hall of Ramses II in the temple of the national god Amun at Karnak. XIXth Dynasty, 1290-1224 B.C. Cf. p. 189.*

of placing the entire temple complex in the interior of the cliff. In front of the rear wall of the forecourt, on either side of the entrance, are two seated figures of Ramses II, hewn out of the rock, each measuring some 20 metres in height. The doorway leads into a huge pillared hall, in which stand 10 colossi of the king in the guise of Osiris. Adjoining this is another pillared hall, and a hall sited at an angle; after this one reaches the holy of holies. This contains the statue of the king, who already during his lifetime was worshipped as divine, and also statues of the gods Amun, Rēhorakhty and Ptah.

The colossi on either side of the entrance and those in the first pillared hall are the most splendid works of the Ramessid period. The proportions have a fine symmetry and the faces are modelled with painstaking care. This monumentality does not preclude a sense of pathos and blends into the rocky surroundings; the towering cliffs make them seem less oppressively heavy than other XIXth Dynasty monumental statues. The axis of the temple is oriented towards the point where the sun rises at the equinox, so that the light of the rising sun can penetrate right into the holy of holies and for a few moments shine upon the statues of the gods, giving them a mysterious glow. A second temple at Abu Simbel is dedicated to the goddess Hathor and to Nefretiri, the consort of Ramses II. At the entrance to the temple, which is likewise built into the rock, there are niches containing six statues of the king and his consort. The monuments which the king built in the Delta and Lower Egypt have not been preserved; and the palace of his successor, Merneptah, at Memphis has also been almost completely destroyed.

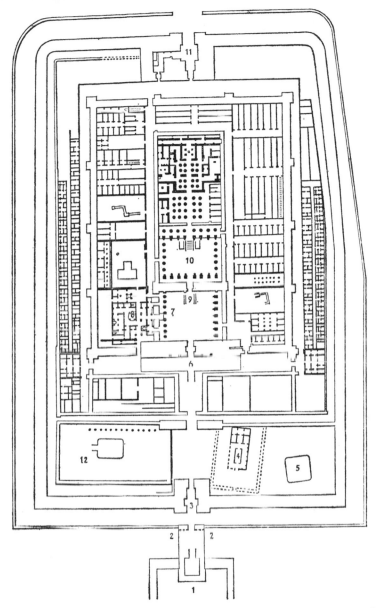

FIG. 59 — *Ground-plan of temple area at Medinet Habu. Age of Ramses III, XXth Dynasty, 1198-1167 B.C. Cf. pp. 192, 215.*

1. *Landing-stage*
2. *External wall*
3. *So-called 'High Gateway'*
4. *XVIIIth Dynasty temple*
5. *Sacred lake*
6. *1st pylon of Ramses III*
7. *Court containing palace facade and windows for public appearances*
8. *Palace of Ramses III*
9. *2nd pylon of Ramses III*
10. *Dwellings of priests and magazines*
11. *West Gate (destroyed)*
12. *Mortuary Temple of Amenardis, XXVth Dynasty*

FIG. 60 — 'High Gateway' of the temple at Medinet Habu. XXth Dynasty, 1198-1167 B.C. Reconstruction. Cf. below

*XXth Dynasty*

Towards the end of the XIXth Dynasty the power of the state declined, and this was reflected in art. It was not checked until the XXth Dynasty, by Ramses III.

The small temple and the Khons Temple at Karnak date from the XXth Dynasty. But the most important example of temple architec-

*FIG. 59*

ture in this period is the temple of Ramses III, which is in a good state of preservation. It is situated on the western bank at Medinet

*Medinet Habu*

Habu, near Thebes. It is the last monumental temple to have been built during the New Kingdom. It resembles a fortress: the entire

*FIG. 60*

temple area is enclosed by a wall, and there are two huge gateways in the east and west. The eastern gate-house consisted of three storeys and had a crenellated wall. It did not serve a warlike purpose: it was here, as is shown by the reliefs in the interior, that the pharaoh amused himself with the ladies of his harem. The imposing pylon at the entrance leads into the open court, which also forms the forecourt of the royal palace to the south; on the southern side of the open court are papyrus columns, and on the northern side Osiride pillars. There was an aperture like a window through which the ruler could step out of the palace on to a balustrade, and show himself to his subjects assembled in the court below. A second pylon leads from the first court into a second columned court, and then to the adjoining Amun Temple, around which are the dwellings of the priests and the administrative buildings.

The XVIIIth Dynasty temple was incorporated into the temple area when the enclosure wall was built. Towards the end of Ramses III's reign a second enclosure wall was put up around the temple area. This enhanced still further its fortress-like aspect.

The royal tombs dating from the XIXth and XXth Dynasties situated in the Valley of the Kings at Thebes are laid out according to the plan customary from the reign of Amenophis IV onwards. They are cut into the rock, in a straight line, and consist of a large number of pillared halls, corridors and small chambers.

*Royal tombs of the Ramessid era*

For the queens and members of the royal family a separate cemetery was built in the 'Valley of the Queens', behind the temple at Medinet Habu. Their tombs were smaller than those of the kings. In most

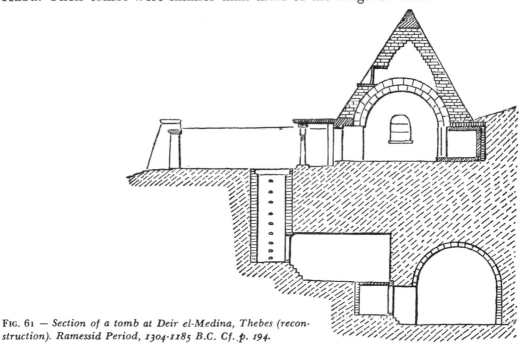

FIG. 61 — *Section of a tomb at Deir el-Medina, Thebes (reconstruction). Ramessid Period, 1304-1185 B.C. Cf. p. 194.*

FIG. 62 — *King Seti I fighting the Hittites. Detail of a limestone relief on the northern external wall of the Hypostyle Hall at Karnak. XIXth Dynasty, 1302-1290 B.C. Cf. p. 195.*

cases they comprise no more than a forecourt, some short corridors and a sarcophagus-chamber.

*Private tombs of the Ramessid era*

The few private tombs at Thebes that have survived usually contain spacious pillared halls. We may single out for attention those of the artisans and workers of the city of the dead, in the cemetery at Deir el-Medina. These consist of a brick pyramid, in the interior of which is a barrel-vaulted offering-room. Several of the subterranean rooms, including the sarcophagus-chamber, have walls and vaulting lined with brick.

FIG. 61

Since the seat of government under the Ramessids was transferred to the Delta, it may be assumed that dignitaries and court officials were also interred in that area. Unfortunately not one of their tombs has come to light.

RELIEF AND PAINTING

Prior to the reign of Thutmosis III only the interior rooms of temples bore carvings in relief. His successors, however, appear to have decorated the external walls of temples as well. These scenes glorified the king as a victor in battle or as a successful hunter. The battle scenes featured on the body of Thutmosis IV's chariot and Tutankhamun's chest are no doubt modelled upon large wall scenes that have since been destroyed.

*Temple reliefs of the XIXth Dynasty*

In temples dating from the XIXth and XXth Dynasties, however, imposing scenes have survived. They depict pitched battles fought by Seti I, Ramses II and Ramses III. They are almost invariably executed in sunk relief, and are carved with an eye to the viewer. They unfurl before him on a grandiose scale lively and dramatic pictures of specific historical events.

In most of these reliefs concern with historical facts and the representation of large bodies of men take precedence over artistic treatment of detail. Those carved by Seti I on the outer face of the north wall of the great Hypostyle Hall at Karnak give a chronological account of his Syrian campaign. The pharaoh is shown in his war-chariot as a victorious leader, driving his enemies before him in a confused and disorderly rout. Some of them have taken refuge in a fortress which is under attack by the Egyptians. Instead of being arranged systematically in different registers, the multiplicity of pictorial detail is brought together to form a spirited composition. Ramses II furnished his temples with huge reliefs recording his campaigns against the Hittites and the famous battle of Kadesh. In the composition just mentioned which was carved by Seti I at Karnak the battle is shown after the outcome had been decided, whereas in those decorating Ramses II's temple the king is shown in the thick of the fray, together with his Egyptian tribes and a force of foreign mercenaries.

The fine reliefs of the Abydos temple depict both the ferocity of the battle and also capture the mood of particular moments in it — its

Fig. 62

FIG. 63 — *Naval battle fought by Ramses III. Detail of sandstone relief in the temple at Medinet Habu. XXth Dynasty, 1198-1167 B.C. Cf. p. 196.*

195

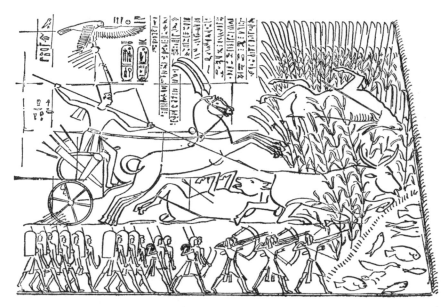

FIG. 64 — *King Ramses III hunting wild bulls. Detail of sandstone relief in the temple at Medinet Habu. XXth Dynasty, 1198-1167 B.C. Cf. below*

grim horrors — in superb detail. Thus the picture of a devastated countryside, with shattered houses and trees, gives an impression of the emptiness and desolation that followed the battle. In the pillared hall of the temple at Abu Simbel the historic battle of Kadesh is depicted on the north wall. On the south wall are consecutive scenes which cannot be assigned to any particular locality or date. In the centre the pharaoh is shown stabbing a Libyan prince; to the left and right he can be seen conquering the Semites and Nubians.

*Temple reliefs of the XXth Dynasty*
The pathos expressed in the battle-scene relief of Ramses II occurs in the murals in Ramses III's temple at Medinet Habu. The northern outside wall features the battle fought against the 'Peoples of the FIG. 63 Sea'. There is an unsurpassed virtuosity in the representation of the fierce turmoil of battle. Enemy soldiers, drowning and dying, are shown in distorted postures. Hunting, too, lent itself to animated scenes with ample dramatic tension. On the outside of the northern FIG. 64 wall of the temple is a scene showing a lion-hunt, and on the rear wall of the first pylon one showing the hunting of wild bulls, wild asses and gazelles. The historical pictures in the Ramessid temples would seem to have been carved with the viewer in mind, considering the pictorial character of the scenes, and the foreshortening and over-

lapping of the spirited figures. But they are placed high up on the temple walls and cannot be made out with the naked eye. Therefore we must conclude that even these lively scenes of specific historical events must actually have been designed for the glorification of the pharaoh and his deeds, without any concern for the spectator.

As well as historical scenes there are also ritual ones. From the standpoint of subject and style they follow the traditional pattern for such works in temples. They repeat with pious solemnity the ancient scenes showing the king worshipping the gods. The fine elaborately worked reliefs of Ramses I and Seti I in the temples at Abydos and the Hypostyle Hall at Karnak still have about them a faint echo of the charming elegant style found in the flowering period of the New Kingdom. The gentle forms and lines of earlier works have been translated into clear-cut outlines. The slender bodies are modelled with assurance, as are the material of the flowing robes, the jewellery and wigs — although here and there, despite all the subtlety employed, there is an occasional touch of mannered coldness.

It was during the Ramessid era in particular that the pharaonic tombs in the Valley of the Kings, with their numerous corridors, stairs and halls, were furnished with scenes illustrating events in the nether world described in the Books of the Dead. Already in the XVIIIth Dynasty the texts of the dead, with their outline drawings, had been transferred to the whitewashed walls of the tombs, giving them the effect of papyrus manuscripts.

The tomb of Seti I constitutes the high-water mark of sepulchral art during the Ramessid period. The colours of the fine reliefs are in an excellent state of preservation. On the door-jamb from his tomb, which is now in Paris, the king is shown appearing before the goddess Hathor. Typical of the refined style developed during the early Ramessid period are the slender figures, the assured elegance of line and colour, and the meticulous representation of garment folds, wigs and jewellery.

FIG. 65

In contrast to the pathos expressed in the battle-scene reliefs those in tombs emanate a restrained beauty and emotional intensity which spring from the revival of religious life at this time.

In the private tombs at Thebes, too, a tendency towards religious subjects is now apparent. Pride of place is taken by scenes showing the cult of the dead, the worshipping of the gods, the funeral procession and the judgment of the dead. The friezes continue from one wall to the next, taking no account of the corners of the room; these

FIG. 65 — *Seti I in the presence of the goddess Hathor. Painted limestone relief on a pillar of his tomb, in the Valley of the Kings at Thebes. New Kingdom, XIXth Dynasty, approx. 1300 B.C. Width 1.20 m. Cf. p. 197.*

FIG. 66    are usually rounded off. The exceedingly gaunt figures have rather small oval heads, and are depicted wearing the fashionable richly-pleated robes of the Ramessid period, with widely-flaring skirts. At times it seems as though more attention is paid to the robes, coiffures, jewellery and sandals than to the human figure itself.

The tombs of the artisans employed at Thebes, the city of the dead, are situated at Deir el-Medina. From an artistic point of view they form a separate group. There is an original carefree vitality and realism in the humorous treatment of subjects and the lovingly exact rendering of plants and animals.

In the Theban tombs painting plays a prominent part, but in Sakkara there are a vast number of Ramessid reliefs which both from the standpoint of motifs and style display the influence of Old Kingdom tombs; the latter were present in large numbers in the cemetery at Sakkara and served as models. Towards the end of the Ramessid period the style of most of the compositions is mannered, rigid and solemn. The colours become matt in tone; the ground is a dull grey and yellow. In the Deir el-Medina tombs the painting is careless and slovenly.

**SCULPTURE IN THE ROUND**    By the XIXth Dynasty, after the spiritual and religious convulsions of the Amarna period, the idea of sacrosanct monarchy had once again become firmly established, and indeed was even stronger than it had been before. The claims of the god-king became so insistent that a statue of the pharaoh came to be considered equivalent to one of a god, and was worshipped already during the king's lifetime.

Hitherto a popular theme in art had been the king under the protection of the gods. Now this was reversed: the god frequently appears under the protection of the king, who is drawn to a much larger scale. In the traditional style of royal sculpture, exemplified by the fine *Royal sculpture* granite statue of Ramses II at Turin, the contour lines are more clear-cut, and stand in contrast to the soft modelling. The sharp FIG. 67 edges of the folds of his robe and the accuracy with which the individual volumes are modelled are almost metallic in their hardness. But the expression of the face, on the other hand, suggests a kind and gentle person, with a spiritual turn of mind.

The motif of the king kneeling to make his offering is modified: var- FIG. 68 ious representations show him cringing on the ground, his figure slender and supple.

When evaluating monumental sculpture, first consideration should be given to the fact that, to a greater extent than with other statuary, it was a constituent part of the architectural scheme of the building in which it was placed, and frequently of the landscape as well. The colossal statue seldom appears on its own. The entrance to the temple at Abu Simbel is accentuated by four imposing seated colossi, which PLATE P. 138 on account of their enormous size can hold their own against the natural grandeur of the mountainous setting.

The statues showing kings leaning against pillars, and also Osiride pillars, serve to emphasize the architectonic articulation of space.

FIG. 66 — *Detail of a scene showing a funeral procession, in the tomb of Roy at Thebes. XIXth Dynasty, 1304-1200 B.C. Cf. p. 204.*

There are several of them, all of the same shape, in the front hall of Abu Simbel; their number corresponds to that of the pillars there. PLATE P. 140 In the temple at Luxor they are placed in each of the spaces between the columns. The precise bold proportioning of monumental sculpture testifies to a high degree of skilled craftsmanship. On the other hand, it is undeniable that, generally speaking, in the case of statues in the round little care was taken with the modelling of detail; the level of technical accomplishment thus surpasses that of the artistic quality. The fact that monumental sculpture serves as an architectural member means that the image loses depth — from a spiritual as well as an artistic point of view. Thus is is not surprising that the Ramessid colossi, when seen in museums divorced from their natural and architectonic setting, should convey a sense of superficiality and pathos, or of rough clumsy workmanship. The finest Ramessid works, such as the seated figures at the entrance of the temple at Abu Simbel, are effective images of the pharaoh.

Under Ramses III the fondness for monumentality and colossal dimensions appears to have decreased. On the other hand royal statues become increasingly rigid and impersonal, and the expression becomes mannered and fatigued.

*Sculpture of private persons* Figures of private persons carry on directly the traditions of the XVIIIth Dynasty. Among the statues in the round that have survived temple statues outnumber by far funerary ones. The favourite form is that of the block-statue, which in its simplicity and compactness seemed most appropriate to the new tendency in the direction of meditation and quiet humble devotion.

Statues of scribes, which had come into vogue already in Old Kingdom times, appear in the most varied modifications. Less importance is now attached to the activity of the scribe than to his facial expression — of introspective meditation.

FIG. 69 Many temple statues of priests are depicted holding a shrine with small idols. These foreshadow the rising power of a self-assertive priesthood. In these statues the priests appear as protectors of the gods.

The traditional standing and seated figures, and also composite scenes, are worked with meticulous care and precision. One cannot but be

FIG. 67 — *Black granite statue of King Ramses II. XIXth Dynasty, 1290-1224 B.C. Museo Egiziano, Turin. Height 1.94 m. Cf. p. 199.*

PLATE 57 — Cat: sacred animal of the goddess Bastet. Bronze with gold ear-rings. Late Period, 7th-6th cents. B.C. *Walters Art Gallery, Baltimore. Height 19.7 cm. Cf. p. 220.*

PLATE 58 — Baboon with an eye-amulet. Light green faience. Late Period, 7th-6th cents. B.C. *Walters Art Gallery, Baltimore. Height 4.75 cm. Cf. p. 220.*

PLATE 59 — Faience vessel. Ptolemaic Period, 1st cent. B.C. *Kestner Museum, Hanover. Height 14 cm.*
*Cf. p. 228.*

PLATE 60 — Portrait head of a priest of the god Month. Green stone. Late Period, XXXth Dynasty, approx. 350 B.C. *Brooklyn Museum, New York, Height 15.3 cm. Cf. p. 221.*


PLATE 61 — Ptolemy I rendering sacrifice to the god Horus. Painted limestone relief. From a chapel of Ptolemy I at Tuna el-Gebel (Hermopolis), Middle Egypt. Ptolemaic Period, approx. 300 B.C. *Pelizaeus* ▶ *Museum, Hildesheim. Cf. p. 226.*

PLATE 62 — The goddess Isis. Painted limestone relief. Ptolemaic Period, 4th cent. B.C. *Kestner Museum, Hanover. Height 44 cm. Cf. p. 227.*

FIG. 68 — *Ramses II humbly making a votive offering. Slate. From Karnak. XIXth Dynasty, 1290-1224 B.C. Egyptian Museum, Cairo. Length 75 cm. Cf. p. 199.*

struck by the accurate, yet often slightly schematized, treatment of the pleated robes, as well as of the wigs and jewellery.

The facial expression is one of extreme refinement and of rigidity. Instead of vitality, there is merely the suggestion of a smile.

Ramessid art grows out of the rich traditions of the XVIIIth Dynasty and occasionally also falls back upon Old and Middle Kingdom motifs and forms. At the same time, however, vigorous new forms develop that conform to the attitude of mind prevalent towards the close of the New Kingdom. The battle-scene relief with its animation and tension, the colossi of Ramses II, and the monumental splendour of the columned halls — all reflect the pretensions to world-power status, which under the Ramessids once again became a reality.

In skilful representation of the human spirit and in mastery of technique Egyptian art now seemed to have reached its apogee. After this there could only be a gradual ossification and disintegration, which by the end of the New Kingdom resulted in a decline.

New Kingdom craft products are of particular opulence and variety. The rich treasure of Tutankhamun (cf. Plate on p. 141), funerary gifts in private tombs, and finds in the ruins of houses at Amarna have yielded a large amount of furniture, household effects and jewellery, which testify to the refined style of life that was possible so long as Egypt was a world power. *Crafts in the New Kingdom*

Red clay vessels decorated with ornamental blue bands and festoons, and faience bowls painted in a turquoise shade and featuring flowers and fish, are to be found alongside alabaster vessels — sometimes nobly proportioned, and sometimes grotesquely overladen with decoration. The four canopic jars in which the viscera of the dead are kept are made of fine-grained alabaster. They are deemed to be under the protection of the spirits of the dead — Amset, Hapi, Duamutef and Kebeh-senuf, sons of the god Horus. The lid, which in the New Kingdom is given the shape of a plastically modelled human head, must PLATE P. 142 PLATE P. 159 PLATE P. 85

be regarded as an image of the deceased. The latter's name and title are recorded in the inscription on the wall of the vessel. On some of these lids from canopic jars the details are treated plastically in such a way as to give them a truly artistic quality. During the Late Period canopic lids take the shape of human heads and also the heads of baboons, jackals or falcons, thereby embodying in symbolic form the four spirits of the dead.

PLATE P. 160    Superb works produced by goldsmiths testify to the technical skill and sense of beauty which these craftsmen possessed. Semi-precious stones, pastes and enamel lend a touch of vitality to the glittering gold.

PLATE P. 161    The colours are delightful. But XIXth Dynasty embossed gold and silver vessels from Zagazig also merit unqualified admiration.

PLATE P. 162    Bronze mirrors, cosmetic jars and unguent-spoons made of wood, stone or ivory in fanciful shapes give proof of the stylistic refinement and wealth of imagination that existed during this era, which was so exposed to stimulation from outside.

ART IN THE LIBYAN PERIOD    Already during the reigns of the last rulers of the Ramessid Dynasty it was evident that the nation's spiritual and artistic powers were beginning to flag and become ossified. These tendencies were enhanced during the transitional era between the New Kingdom and the Late Period. Most of the sparse relics of artistic products that have survived from the era between the XXIst and XXIVth Dynasties (approx. 1185-712 B.C.) are related to those from the Ramessid period, and may thus be considered as belonging to the final phase of the New Kingdom. New techniques are developed, and one can note the beginnings of artistic trends that were to become characteristic of the Late Period. This intermediate era thus foreshadows the final section of Egyptian history, the age of foreign domination.

The XXIst Dynasty completed the Khons Temple at Karnak, the building of which had begun under Ramses III. The founder of the XXIInd Dynasty, the Libyan king Sheshonk I, added to the temple at Karnak the so-called Bubastide Hall, in front of the Hypostyle Hall of Ramses II. A new architectural idea, which was taken up again later during the Ptolemaic period, is evident in the small temple to Amun at El Hibe, in Middle Egypt, built by Sheshonk I. The court was enclosed by walls between the columns, which were half the normal height. Both temple architecture and reliefs in temples are linked stylistically to the architecture and reliefs of the Ramessid period.

The most important accomplishment of the Libyan period was perhaps the production of large bronze figures. These showed a high degree of technical skill. Inlaying of metals in the metallic ground and engraving were popular means of adding a touch of life to the surface of the figures. This extended down to the very last detail. Inlays of electrum, silver, semi-precious stones, pastes and glass, or a layer of gold-leaf were used to give the bronzes colour and charm. The graceful statue of Karomama, the consort of one of the Libyan kings from the XXIInd Dynasty, exemplifies the high level of tech- PLATE P. 181 nical perfection and the fine sense of form that were evident in the bronze sculpture of this period.

Private sculpture is almost exclusively confined to two types: the person making offerings and the block-statue. They were decorated with reliefs and inscriptions.

The growing tendency to draw upon older works, adding to them inscriptions relevant to the age in which they were made, foreshadows the custom of the Late Period, when exact copies were made of ancient works. In the Libyan era artists lacked sufficient talent to develop an individual style of their own, related to the times in which they lived, and it was for this reason that works made in the past were simulated. The Libyans took their models from the statuary of the Middle Kingdom, which they frequently copied without making any modification whatsoever.

# XII. LATE PERIOD

HISTORICAL
SURVEY
The final segment of Egyptian history, the Late Period, is pre-eminently an era of alien domination. It begins with the rule of the Nubians, whom the Greeks called Ethiopians. They claimed the throne of the pharaohs as the XXVth Dynasty.

MAP P. 235
During the period of Libyan rule Nubia had thrown off the Egyptian yoke and formed an independent kingdom. Its capital was at Napata, near the Fourth Cataract. Egypt's influence upon her former province was evident in the cultural field, particularly in the adoption of the Amun cult. The Nubians regarded themselves as the upholders and true heirs of this cult. It is possible that the first step they took was to lay claim to the principal temple dedicated to Amun at Thebes — a claim which may have found support among the priests of the temple at Karnak, who had emigrated to Nubia during the time of troubles. In 750 B.C. Kashta, a Nubian, conquered the southern part of Upper Egypt, including Thebes.

From the early XVIIIth Dynasty onwards the rich treasures of the Amun Temple at Thebes were in the hands of a priestess of royal blood. King Kashta of Ethiopia forced the priestess who belonged to the Libyan Dynasty to adopt his daughter Amenardis. All the kings of the XXVth and XXVIth Dynasties followed suit, in order to strengthen the connection between themselves and the temple property — and all the power that this implied.

*Ethiopian rule*
*712-633 B.C.*
In 721 B.C. the Ethiopians also succeeded in taking Memphis, and in 712 B.C. King Shabaka put an end to the dynasty in the Delta, which had retained its independence up to that time. This marked the beginning of Ethiopian rule, which was to last until 663 B.C. The Ethiopian Empire was exposed to the danger of attack by the Assyrians, who were then at the zenith of their power. The Assyrian army, under the command of King Sennacherib, was at first victorious, but then plague broke out and it was compelled to retreat before reaching the borders of Egypt. However, not long afterwards, in 670 B.C., King Esarhaddon conquered Egypt, which for seven years became an Assyrian province.

The last king of the XXVth Dynasty, Tanutamun, only held sway over Upper Egypt. His attempt to regain control of Lower Egypt led to the destruction of Thebes by Assur-bani-pal, king of Assyria, who was in occupation of the northern part of the country.

In the course of the conflicts and disturbances that took place during the Ethiopian era Prince Necho of Saïs, in the Delta, was taken as a prisoner to Nineveh in connection with a conspiracy to which he was a party, together with King Taharka of Ethiopia, against Assyrian rule. He gained the confidence of Assur-bani-pal, who bestowed upon him the title of King of Egypt, and then returned to his country. Necho was killed by King Tanutamun of Ethiopia, and his son Psammetichus thereupon fled to the Assyrians. The latter restored him to power, not only in his own principality, but in Memphis as well. Psammetichus was a shrewd politician, and succeeded in making Egypt once more an independent state, with a native dynasty. In 663 B.C. he founded the XXVIth Dynasty, also known (after its capital at Saïs, in the Delta) as the Saite Dynasty.

When the peaceful reign of Psammetichus I came to an end, his son Necho undertook a campaign against the Syrians. He hoped to bring to pass the old dream of an Egyptian world empire, which had never been given up entirely. He succeeded in defeating the Israelite king Josiah near Megiddo and conquered Syria, but then suffered a crushing defeat near Carchemish on the Euphrates at the hands of Nebuchadnezzar, as a result of which all the territories he had conquered were once again lost.

Psammetichus II is also recorded as having made an unsuccessful attempt to subjugate Lower Nubia. During his reign Greek merchants and colonists were granted permission to settle in Egypt. His son Apries (the Hophra of the Old Testament) made another effort to realize his father's ambitions in Asia. He concluded an alliance with the king of Israel against Nebuchadnezzar, but was unable to prevent the Babylonians from conquering Jerusalem and taking the Israelites into captivity. He returned to Egypt without having achieved anything. At home disorders broke out; Apries was deposed, and one of his military commanders, Amasis, was proclaimed king. Amasis legitimized his accession to the throne by marrying one of Psammetichus II's daughters.

Amasis was shrewd and well versed in world affairs. Herodotus refers to him as a great friend of the Greeks. He maintained a close amicable relationship with Polycrates of Samos.

In the meantime the political scene in Asia Minor had changed. King Cyrus of Persia had destroyed the kingdom of Lydia and conquered Babylon. The consolidation of the Persian Empire prevented Amasis from attempting to reconquer territory in Syria. On the other hand, he was able to lay the foundations of Egyptian sea-power. Her navy continued to play an important role until the Ptolemaic era. The reign of his son, Psammetichus III, lasted for a mere six months. In 525 B.C. a Persian army under Cambyses, son of Cyrus, defeated the Egyptians near Pelusium, in the north-eastern part of the Delta. Psammetichus was put to death. This brought to a close the history of Egypt as an independent state. The land on the Nile now became a satrapy of the Persian Empire. This was ruled by the Achaemenids, who are reckoned as the XXVIIth Dynasty. All Egypt's efforts to shake off the Persian yoke were thwarted. In 460 B.C. Athens gave its support to a revolt by bringing her fleet to bear, but this venture also came to nought.

During the 4th century B.C. Amyrtaeus of Saïs succeeded in ridding Egypt of the Persians and ascended the throne of the pharaohs himself. He and his descendants are reckoned as the XXVIIIth Dynasty. This was succeeded by another dynasty, the XXIXth, composed of princes from Mendes, in the eastern part of the Delta.

The XXXth Dynasty, comprising Kings Nectanebo I, Tacho, and Nectanebo II, from Sebennythos in the central part of the Delta, brings to an end the sequence of dynasties recorded in the lists of kings. In 341 B.C. King Artaxerxes III reconquered Egypt and once again turned it into a Persian satrapy until 332 B.C., when it was occupied by Alexander the Great after a bloodless campaign. Soon after his conquest of Egypt Alexander founded the city of Alexandria, which soon developed into a centre of international commerce and one of the principal strongholds of Greek culture.

After his death in 323 B.C. his military commander Ptolemy won domination over Egypt. At first he reigned as proxy to the heirs of Alexander the Great, Philip Arrhidaeus and Alexander II. Later he ruled the country in his own right, as an independent king. After his death he was accorded divine honours and the cognomen 'Sotêr' (= Saviour). He is the founder of the Ptolemaic Dynasty which, during the three centuries for which it held sway, made Egypt the most prosperous state in the world. But towards the end of this era civil strife once again broke out.

Cleopatra, the last ruler of the Ptolemaic dynasty, sought Caesar's protection against her brother. With his support she was restored to the throne, and her son Caesarion appointed co-regent. When, on the death of Caesar, Antonius was sent from Rome to attack her, she succeeded in exercising such a powerful influence over him that he found himself arraigned in the Roman Senate as a traitor. In 30 B.C., after Octavius won the naval battle of Actium, Cleopatra and Antonius committed suicide and Egypt became a Roman province.

At the beginning of the 2nd century A.D. Christianity spread throughout Egypt, bringing a new spiritual and artistic outlook in its train. The Coptic Church came into being and monasteries were founded.

*Roman rule*

The Libyans and Ethiopians became so permeated with Egyptian culture that they had some justification in regarding themselves as descendants of the ancient pharaohs, and taking over the political functions of the great rulers of the New Kingdom. But under the Assyrians and Persians Egypt was merely a provincial outpost, and under Greek and Roman rule the country became part of their respective empires.

*Monarchy*

The characteristic feature of the Late Period is the strong ties that were maintained with the traditions of the great epochs of the past. Both the Ethiopian kings and the Persian emperors, and also the Ptolemies and Romans, built new temples dedicated to the Egyptian gods. They had themselves represented on temple walls in the garb and attitude of the ancient pharaohs, worshipping the same deities that they had once worshipped. The king was now seen as no more than an earthly ruler, who maintained the divinely sanctioned order.

The influence of the priesthood on political life increased from the XXIst Dynasty onwards owing to the introduction of the Oracle of Amun, which made pronouncements on political as well as religious questions. The fact that their offices had become hereditary helped to consolidate the influence of the Amun priests.

*Priesthood*

In the army, too, a hereditary warrior caste developed. The same tendency could be observed in other professions. Gradually all initiative and freedom were stifled by the weight of tradition.

*Army*

From literary texts and inscriptions on statues it is possible to gain an insight into the enlightened attitude of mind to be found among members of the upper classes at this time. Their outlook was based neither on religious dogmas, nor on magic or mythological concepts. Instead they developed a sceptical intellectual way of thinking. They believed that the gods dispensed their blessings according to the ethical conduct of the individual. Virtue did not, however, necessarily result in reward by the gods, for their will was unpredictable. This attitude of mind had two consequences. On one hand it led to doubt

*Thought*

about the prospect of a happy life beyond the grave. On the other hand it led to an awareness that each individual ought to act responsibly, and ensure the immortality of his name by living according to ethical norms and performing good deeds. This outlook was confined *Popular beliefs* to the upper strata of society. The broad masses adhered to the religious concepts that had been part of Egyptian life for millennia. With the collapse of political unity the importance of the old national god, Amun, decreased, and the ancient local gods regained prestige. A syncretism developed whereby a distinction ceased to be drawn between their individual qualities and functions. A particular feature was the revival of the tendency to worship sacred animals, which had never completely died out.

Information about the various animal cults that existed can be gleaned from the accounts of Greek and Roman visitors to Egypt. "Many people justly find very curious and remarkable the customs connected with sacred animals," wrote Diodorus Siculus in the 1st century A.D. "For the Egyptians worship some animals beyond all measure — both alive and dead. If one of these animals dies it is wrapped in a shroud and carried off to the embalming-place, the mourners beating their chests and lamenting. The body of the dead animal is anointed with cedar oil and treated with various scents and other substances to preserve it, and is then interred in a grave."

PLATE P. 179 A special role was played by the cult of the sacred Apis bull at Memphis. It was consulted as an oracle well into the Christian era.

The religious views of the people were limited to a rigid adherence to traditional forms, the content of which they were sometimes no longer able to interpret.

Particularly characteristic of the Late Period is the tendency towards magic — the product of doubts about the prospects of an after-life. Protective amulets and various magic formulae were thought capable of protecting men from evil forces and securing the intervention of the gods on their behalf. In the Late Period men's lives were governed by extremes: on one hand, an open-minded ethical attitude, on the other an adherence to the externals of a tradition that had become petrified. This duality is also evident in the art of this era.

# XIII. ART AND ARCHITECTURE
## IN THE LATE PERIOD

To the state temple of the god Amun at Karnak the Ethiopians added ARCHITECTURE the great pylon that still stands there today, walling off the huge court *Temples* built during the XXIInd Dynasty. A papyrus column, some 27 metres FIG. 37 high, which is also still standing, is a relic of the kiosk which King Taharka built in the large court during the Libyan era.

The Ethiopians also added a pylon to the temple at Medinet FIG. 59 Habu.

Their kings were buried in their native Nubia, but the priestess Amenardis, who was of royal blood, was interred at Thebes. Her mortuary chapel is situated between the tall gateway and the first pylon at Medinet Habu. It comprises a columned court and a barrel-vaulted offering-room with ancillary chapels.

After the Assyrian invasions the importance of Thebes receded into *Tombs of private persons* the background to such an extent that no major architectural elements were added to the huge Amun temple complex. Little has survived in the way of monuments from the XXVIth Dynasty in the Delta area. On the other hand, there are several private tombs with huge brick superstructures in the city of the dead at Thebes, on the western bank of the river. The sequence of subterranean sepulchral chambers and pillared halls in this extensive complex is reminiscent of that in the royal tombs of the XVIIIth Dynasty.

During the reigns of the Persian kings of the XXVIIth Dynasty a temple to Amun was built at the oasis of Khârga. The great agglomeration of ruins at Bahbit el-Higara, called by the Romans the 'Iseum' on account of the Isis sanctuary situated there, is a relic of the extensive building programme carried on under the XXXth Dynasty. Kings of these dynasties also built temples at several places in Upper Egypt. They are characterized by the fine, elaborately conceived proportions of their architectural members, which in the main follow the pattern established in the XXVIIIth Dynasty. The similarities are evident in the papyrus-bundle columns in the vestibule at Medinet Habu, erected in front of the XXVth Dynasty pylon, which have stalks with three sides, worked in a naturalistic style. These resemble Amenophis III's fine columns in the temple at Luxor. The motifs and styles of the temple reliefs of the Ethiopian era are in accordance with

Fig. 70 — *Bee-keeping. Detail of limestone relief in the tomb of Pubes at Thebes. XXVIth Dynasty, 664-525 B.C. Cf. p. 217.*

traditional schematic principles. The king is shown worshipping the gods; battle scenes no longer occur.

**RELIEF AND PAINTING** Information about reliefs and paintings during the Ethiopian and Saite periods can be gleaned from the reliefs in the sepulchral palaces at Thebes. Their subjects, and the arrangement of the figures, follow the traditions of the Old, Middle and New Kingdoms, but the mode of rendering details such as robes and coiffures accords with the fashion of the times. These are fine scenes, in many cases elaborately worked. One can perceive the break between the stylistic tendencies of the past, which had their origin in a completely different attitude of mind, and the external attributes derived from the age when they were produced. Thus the sure draughtsmanship usually appears a little stiff and artificial, lacking in spiritual content.

In the tomb of Mentemhet scenes occur which were copied from representations in the Mortuary Temple of Hatshepsut at Deir el-Bahari. In the tomb of Iby there are motifs adapted from the tomb, at Deir el-Gebrawi, of a namesake who lived during the VIth Dynasty. Petamenophis had his sepulchral palace decorated with mythological scenes inspired by those in New Kingdom royal tombs.

As well as such representations, in which the influence of the past is clearly discernible, there occurs in the tomb of Pubes a scene taken FIG. 70 from daily life, not based on any known earlier prototype. It depicts an apiary. The forms and proportions are clumsy and lacking in assurance.

A special group comprises a number of reliefs that have only a single register on the block-like plane, in which all the figures face one way. All the reliefs of this group, extending in time from the late XXVIth Dynasty to the early Ptolemaic period, are topped by rounded staves. In most of them the style follows that of the Old Kingdom; so, too, do the texts and calligraphy of the inscriptions.

The contribution made by the Late Period is, once again, to have added details that were currently in vogue, and possibly also to have made more flexible the disposition of the figures on the plane. Among the works in this group special mention must be made of the Tigrane FIG. 71 Relief, now housed in the Alexandria Museum. It takes its name from its former owner. It was produced during the middle of the 4th century B.C., during the XXXth Dynasty. It shows a blind harpist, and women dancing and making music before the occupant of the tomb. The Tigrane Relief was inspired by a subject frequently treated in the tombs of the XVIIIth Dynasty. A delightful new individual style has been developed in the formal treatment of this traditional theme. The fashionable coiffure and robes, beneath which one can detect the rounded volumes of the body, give this scene vitality. It is hard to say to what extent Greek influences are reflected in the Tigrane Relief and similar works. In any case Greek art was already known in Egypt during the XXXth Dynasty.

The clearest impression of the artistic accomplishments of the Ethiop- SCULPTURE IN THE ROUND

FIG. 71 — *Harpist and musicians. Detail of a limestone relief known as the Tigrane Relief after its former owner. From the tomb of Zanofer at Memphis. 4th cent. B.C. Greek and Roman Museum, Alexandria. Cf. above*

FIG. 72 — *Green slate statue of Hawara, the steward of the sacerdotal princess Amenardis. From Karnak. XXVth Dynasty, 712-665 B.C. Egyptian Museum, Cairo. Height 45 cm. Cf. below*

ian period and the following era may be gained from an examination of figures in the round. These have survived in relatively large numbers. The archaizing tendencies of the Late Period are also felt in plastically modelled figures.

*Royal sculpture* King Taharka, for example, is shown in the usual striding posture, leaning against a pillar to his rear, and wearing a short royal kilt. On cursory inspection this statue appears to bear a startling resemblance to Old Kingdom figures made about two thousand years earlier. [30] But when one studies them more attentively a number of differences become apparent, (although the external scheme remains archaic), which show that the Ethiopian era had new stimuli of its own to contribute: the lustre of the polished surface of the hard stone, which was the principal material used; and stylistic features, such as the treatment of the body, and in particular the facial features.

The great achievement of the Late Period is to have created a new and highly realistic human likeness. King Taharka is shown with Negroid features, which indicate the racial origin of the Nubian rulers.

*Sculpture of private persons* A striking fact about figures of private persons is the keen observation of all characteristic features. The temple statues of high officials, where they do not simply copy some ancient scheme, attempt an

*FIG. 72* individual portrait of the personage concerned, far more naturalistic than anything known hitherto. The ugliness of old age is expressed with stark realism by flabby corpulence, limp breasts, and a furrowed weary face, with the nose flat and fleshy. This realism is in conformity with the individualistic and intellectual outlook of the upper classes. The archaizing style expresses the attitude of the priesthood and the broad mass of the people, who regarded the maintenance of tradition as the essence of all things.

In the Old Kingdom, that great epoch of creative vitality, the characteristic theme was youth — eternal and timeless. In the Late Period preference is given to the portrayal of old age — frequently shown as endowed with critical intelligence, and occasionally with a caustic air of superiority.

In the case of female statuettes slender maidenly delicacy gives way to the stumpiness and corpulence typical of Nubian women.

An ivory statuette of a lady of the royal family, now in Edinburgh, PLATE P. 180 depicts her as thickset and plump. The face, with full lips and heavy eyelids, betrays her Negroid racial origin.

In the tombs of Ethiopian kings who ruled over Nubia we find jewellery of exquisite beauty and a high level of technical expertise. A bronze mirror dating from the Shabaka period has a precious gold PLATE P. 182 handle in the shape of a palm column, topped by uraeus serpents, with four deities in high relief around the shaft. It bears a striking resemblance to the handle of a mirror discovered in the tomb of the first king of the IIIrd Ethiopian dynasty in Nubia; in this case there is a papyrus column instead of a palm column, and it is worked in silver.

Under the native XXVIth Dynasty the archaizing tendency became SAITE PERIOD stronger. This return to a glorious past was certainly favoured by the *Sculpture of* restoration of independence, after half a century of Ethiopian rule. *private persons* It led to an idealized traditional style.

The material used was a dark green and black hard stone. It was polished smooth, which gave it an impression of coldness. Faces worked without depth, with the eyebrows straight and narrow, the mouth upturned at the corners, and a narrow chin suggestive of youth — all these features are reminiscent of the idealized image of Old Kingdom times. Nevertheless the formal harmony cannot conceal the fact that Saïte statuary lacks the element of buoyancy which comes from a creative dialogue with nature, and which affords the likeness a certain energy and vitality. The mask-like smile veils a spiritual vacuum.

The museums of the world have in their possession an abundance of *Bronze statuettes* bronzes of animals and deities, which were originally no doubt offerings made in Egyptian temples. Most of these votive gifts are mass-produced figures. They display a fairly high level of craftsmanship, owing to the fact that they carried on the old workshop tradition, and were executed with superb technical expertise. There are also a large number of statues showing the god Osiris and his consort PLATE P. 183 Isis with Horus the child. The representations of sacred animals bear witness to a keen observation of nature, such as had also been manifest PLATES PP. 184 201 in earlier periods. Statuettes of cats and falcons reproduce in a superb manner the nature of the animals concerned. Bronzes made by the hollow-casting method served as coffins for mummified animals. During the Late Period extensive cemeteries were built for them. Occasionally various materials were used to make a work of sculpture. FRONTISPIECE In the case of the ibis, the sacred bird of Thoth, the god of wisdom, the legs and beak are usually of bronze, while the body is worked in gilded wood or alabaster. The ibis was often represented in conjunction with the goddess of truth and justice, Maat. The latter was portrayed in human form, wearing a feather (the hieroglyph for truth) on her head.

Animal figures of stone and faience also exemplify the magnificent skill with which artists managed to capture the characteristics of the animals they represented. The arrogant and superior air of the ba- PLATE P. 202 boon is rendered with the same compelling force as the lissom suppleness of the cat, or the royal majesty of the falcon. These sacred animals also appear on painted wooden coffins. Thus, for example, a young Apis bull was painted on the bottom plank of a coffin now PLATE P. 179 housed in the Pelizaeus Museum, Hildesheim.

XXVIIth-XXXth
Dynasties The Persian rulers who are reckoned as the XXVIIth Dynasty exerted no influence upon the development of Egyptian art. However, during the last three native dynasties important works of art were once again produced. The high-water mark is reached with the works made during the XXXth Dynasty, which owed a great deal to the XVIIIth Dynasty so far as their style and spiritual content were concerned. The perfect smoothness of the polished surface is a characteristic feature of statues in the round during the Late Period; in the statuary of the XXXth Dynasty it is to be found in conjunction with a tendency to rigidity and a formal expression. There is a frightening spiritual vacuum in the unlined face with the frozen smile and high forehead, which only acquires a touch of animation through the lustre of the polished surface. Devoid of inner content, the idealized human likeness that once expressed the spiritual and religious ideals of ancient Egypt has degenerated into a hard sterile formula.

One may also mention in this connection a smaller group consisting *Sculpture of private persons* of heads of private statues. Most of them are worked in a dark green hard stone. Here a new attempt has been made to treat the human countenance in a realistic manner. The first effort to represent anatomically the bone structure of the head may be assigned to the XXXth Dynasty. Most of the so-called 'green heads' that have sur- PLATE P. 204 vived, however, were probably not made until Ptolemaic times. The portrait head of an unknown priest in the service of the god Month suggests an individual with a distinct personality.

Beneath the flat modelling of the broad face one can sense the bone structure. The clearly defined eyebrows, the narrow bridge of the nose, and the closed thin lips give the face a stern independent expression. The half-opened eyes and inflated nostrils, on the other hand, suggest a sensitive mind engrossed in spiritual contemplation.

In this head, as with the Tigrane Relief, produced at the same time (approximately in the middle of the 4th century B.C.), a novel artistic conception makes itself felt. Later it was developed further and finally, under the influence of Greek art, reaches perfection in the works of the Ptolemaic period.

In the political sphere the transition to this era occurred without military conflict. Similarly, no breach of continuity occurs in artistic development. The Ptolemaic period is inspired by spiritual experiences similar to those familiar to men under the last independent Egyptian dynasties.

# XIV. ART AND ARCHITECTURE DURING
# THE PTOLEMAIC AND ROMAN PERIODS

ARCHITECTURE

It was a shrewd political move for the Ptolemaic rulers to present themselves as legitimate successors to the ancient pharaohs, and to show understanding and respect for the religious views and customs of the local population. The Romans also adhered to this wise policy of restraint.

By actively promoting the construction of buildings and making generous donations to temples the foreign rulers won over the priesthood. Under their rule Egyptian art went through a rich second flowering. During the last centuries prior to the dawn of the Christian era it reached the final limits of expression that its spiritual basis permitted.

Particularly interesting are the huge temples erected on the site of older sanctuaries, although there are also a number of smaller buildings as well. The Horus Temple at Edfu, in the southern part of Upper Egypt, is in an excellent state of preservation. It was begun by Ptolemy III Euergetes in 273 B.C. and not completed until 57 B.C. In layout it follows that of the New Kingdom temples, differing only in that two small vestibules have been added. The use of traditional forms testifies to the Ptolemaic architects' perspicacity and aesthetic sense. The growth of the Isis cult during the Late Period led to the addition to the temples of a so-called 'birth house', dedicated to the Mother Goddess. It was here that she was deemed to have given birth to her son. The Ptolemaic era was not productive of new architectural ideas, and only introduced a few new characteristic details.

It now became customary to shut off the large court from the first vestibule by means of balustrades, half the normal height, placed between the columns. This feature has already been noted in the Amun Temple at El Hibe, built during the XXIInd Dynasty.

A novel feature in the Ptolemaic period are the fine composite capitals of columns, in the shape of luxuriant clusters of plants of various kinds. The wealth of imagination manifest in these ever-changing forms stands in contrast to the column-shafts of the Ramessid era, which were covered all over with scenes and inscriptions. The change shows the highly developed sense of pattern and ornamentation that existed in Ptolemaic times.

*Temple at Edfu*

FIGS. 73, 74

FIG. 75

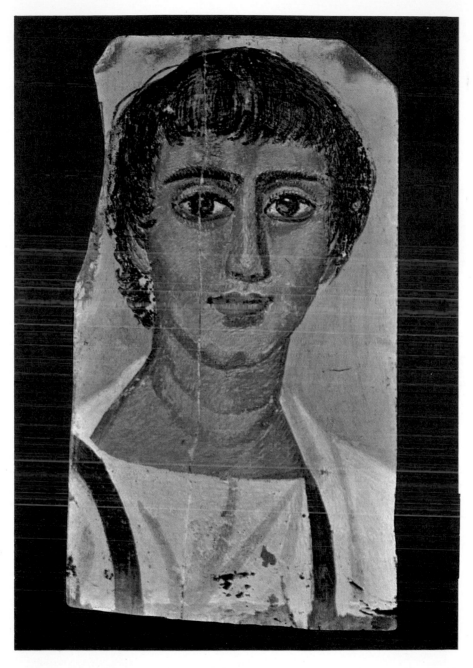

PLATE 63 — Mummy portrait of a young man. Wax-colours on wood. From the Faiyum. 4th cent. B.C. *Kestner Museum, Hanover. Height 35.5 cm. Cf. p 229.*

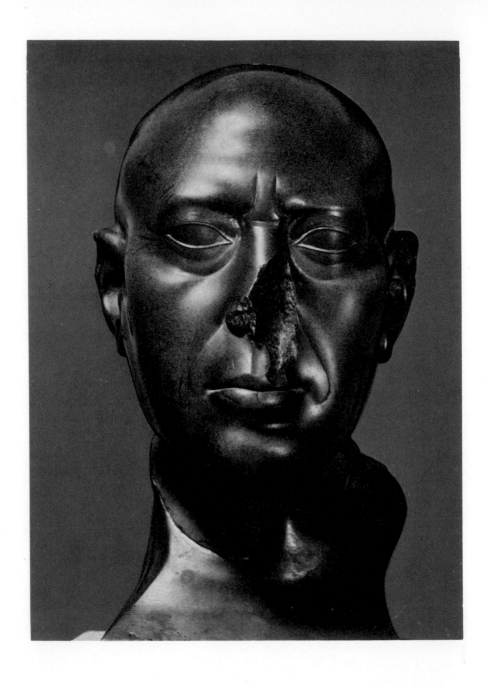

PLATE 64 — Head of a priest, so-called 'Green Head'. Green stone. Ptolemaic Period, 1st cent. B.C. *Former National Museums, Berlin. Height 21 cm. Cf. p. 231.*

The temple at Edfu is in a perfect state of preservation, which enables us to gain an idea of what it must have felt like to be inside an Egyptian temple.

The Hathor Temple at Dendera was begun under the last Ptolemaic *Dendera* rulers and completed in the reign of Emperor Augustus. It took the *FIG. 76* place of an older sanctuary at this site. To support the architrave use was made principally of the four-sided Hathor column. This was also much favoured in the Isis Temple on the island of Philae. The *Philae* opulent temple complexes that were built on this island during Ptolemaic and Roman times are now below the surface of a large reservoir, and are only visible in midsummer, when the level of the water falls.

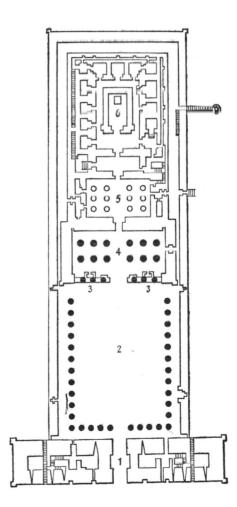

FIG. 73 — *Ground-plan of Horus Temple at Edfu. Ptolemaic Period, 237-147 B.C. 1. Pylon. 2. Court. 3. Columns with intervening balustrades. 4. Vestibule. 5. Hypostyle hall. 6. Sanctuary. Cf. p. 222.*

FIG. 74 — *Vertical section of Horus Temple at Edfu. Entrance to the vestibule. Ptolemaic Period , 237-147 B.C. Cf. p. 222.*

At Kom Ombo a double temple was erected by the Ptolemies in honour of Sobek and Haroeris, two gods who were worshipped at this site. A temple was also planned at Esna, for the ram-headed god Khnum, but only its vestibule was actually built.

Of the temples that were constructed at this time in Lower Nubia nothing has been preserved. The same may be said of the monuments in the Faiyum, in the environs of Memphis, and in the Delta, of which only a few vestiges are left. On the other hand, a good impression of temple architecture in ancient Egypt is given by the temples of Upper Egypt that date from Ptolemaic and Roman times, for these have been well preserved.

**RELIEF AND PAINTING**

*Reliefs in temples*

Just as temple architecture follows New Kingdom models, without adopting any Greek or Roman influences, so also the decoration on the temple walls is governed by tradition. The reliefs show ritual acts in a schematized form. We see row upon row of Ptolemaic and Roman rulers, wearing the traditional costume of the ancient pharaohs, aping their gestures, and worshipping their gods.

PLATE P. 205

Scenes of earthly life, such as the magnificent New Kingdom battle or hunting scenes, no longer have a place in temple art. The endless sequences of cult scenes, accompanied by explanatory inscriptions, are monotonously uniform and lacking in expressiveness. The regular arrangement of panels subdivided by scrolls gives them an almost ornamental character. Although the subjects and arrangement were governed by tradition, a new style was developed which at times

*Reliefs in private tombs*

lent them a noble vigour and elegance. The volumes of the body are treated with greater plasticity and animation than had previously been the case in Egyptian art, and the meticulous handling of detail suggests a fine consciousness of form.

The Kestner Museum, Hanover, possesses a representation of the goddess Isis, depicted with a falcon head. The breasts are modelled fully, and the face is also treated plastically, resulting in a rounded form. PLATE P. 206

The new style of reliefs under Ptolemaic rule could develop more freely in private tombs than it could in temples. At Tuna el-Gebel, near Hermopolis in Middle Egypt, a tomb has been discovered belonging to Petosiris, a high priest of the god Thoth. It was built towards the end of the 4th century B.C., and is in the shape of a small temple. There is an open columned vestibule with low balustrades and a pillared hall, from which a shaft leads into the sarcophagus-chamber.

The vestibule is decorated with scenes of everyday life executed in a curious hybrid Graeco-Egyptian style. The religious scenes in the pillared hall, on the other hand, are conceived in a purely Egyptian style. FIG. 77

In those scenes that represent everyday life the old forms were modified to conform to the fashion of the times. Motifs hitherto unknown,

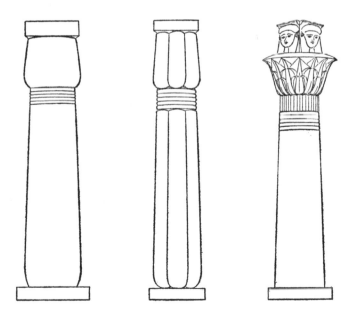

FIG. 75 — *Different types of column and pillar. Cf. pp. 187, 222.*

*Papyrus column, Ramessid Period*

*Composite capital, Ptolemaic Period*

*Hathor capital, New Kingdom — Ptolemaic Period*

227

FIG. 76 — *Vertical section of facade of Hathor Temple at Dendera. Ptolemaic and Roman Period. Cf. p. 225.*

such as threshing corn or turning a lathe, appear for the first time. These scenes are drawn from contemporary life, and the robes and coiffures of the individual figures also reproduce Ptolemaic styles and fashions.

ROMAN PERIOD

Thus scenes depicting life on earth are conceived in a hybrid Graeco-Egyptian style, which accords with the actual coexistence of these two great cultures in Egypt at this time. Ritual scenes, on the other hand, which were alien to the Greeks' way of thinking and sense of form, had to be represented in the ancient Egyptian style. This is proof of a schism that clearly foreshadows the end of ancient Egyptian culture, which had become outmoded.

The Greek and Roman elements appear in a more pronounced form in the scenes in the catacombs at Alexandria, dating from the 2nd century A.D. In this case even the Egyptian gods retain no more than their animal heads, and are clad according to the fashion of the day: Horus, for example, is portrayed as a Roman legionary. In Roman terracottas Egyptian influence is restricted — apart from representations of Horus the child — to attributes that suggest Egyptian deities and symbols.

PLATE P. 203

Ptolemaic faience vessels had thick walls and retained the fine green and blue glaze of former times. They bear friezes in relief showing plants and animals, which anticipate Coptic art both in their naturalistic treatment and in their fine sense of harmony in the ornamentation. Foreigners who lived in Egypt while it was part of the Roman Empire took over the custom of mummifying the dead. Since these sarcophagi, with their monotonous stiff faces, were not in conformity with the taste of the age, faces were painted in the manner

*Portraits on mummies*

of portraits; alternatively, a plaster mask was made to preserve the facial features of the deceased, and this was then wrapped into the bandages enclosing the mummy. Of greater significance from an artistic point of view are the many portraits painted with wax-colours on wood. Most of them were discovered in the Faiyum. They almost PLATE P. 223 invariably represent foreign peoples, especially Greeks and Romans, but also Semites and members of hybrid races. They date from a period extending from the 1st to the 4th centuries A.D. The mummy portraits, which reflect the Egyptian world-outlook, are at the same time the earliest examples of portrait-painting conceived in the Graeco-Roman spirit.

So far as conventional sculpture was concerned, Ptolemaic rule at first made no significant changes. Neither royal statues nor the various types of private figures show any striking difference from those of the Late Period. Only gradually does a new spirit enter into the traditional schemes, making for looser and more naturally rounded forms. The delicate suppleness of women's bodies and the compassionate majesty expressed in the faces occasionally break through the stiff traditional form. In the volumes of the body only a faint tendency can be detected towards an organic vitality, inspired by Greek ideals, and they retain much of their old rigidity. But the faces, on the other hand, are executed in a spirited manner that reflects Greek influences. This development, whereby Greek and Roman elements are juxtaposed without blending, may be observed most clearly in the statues of Ptolemaic rulers.

**SCULPTURE IN THE ROUND**

In figures of private persons the way had already been prepared for new spiritual attitudes by the close of the Late Period. There is an increased expressiveness in the portrait heads which accords with the spirit of early Greek and Hellenistic culture. But the volumes of the body, even when concealed beneath fashionable Greek robes, continue to be limited by Egyptian forms right up to Roman times. It is

*Sculpture of private persons*

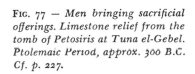

FIG. 77 — *Men bringing sacrificial offerings. Limestone relief from the tomb of Petosiris at Tuna el-Gebel. Ptolemaic Period, approx. 300 B.C. Cf. p. 227.*

| Rē | Amun-Rē | Thoth |
| Hathor | Isis | Anubis |
| Osiris | Ptah | Khnum |

FIG. 78 — *The most important Egyptian gods, in their stylized form. Cf. p. 42.*

only then that Egyptian style disintegrates — particularly in statues of Isis, or of priests and priestesses.

One of the most magnificent works which Egyptian art produced at the end of its long and fruitful course of development is the 'Green Head', in the Former National Museums, Berlin. This head combines the Egyptian talent for natural observation, artistically translated into a line that is almost ornamental, and a late Hellenistic-Roman spiritual content. The powerful head is bald, and one can sense the presence of the bones under the skin. The lines and wrinkles at the corners of the eyes and the top of the nose are represented with calligraphic precision. There are sagging bags under the eyes and grooves running from the nostrils to the corners of the mouth, giving the face a distinct individual cachet. Severity of ornamental detail is combined with a realistic likeness, resulting in a homogeneous portrait. The subject seems to be a man of lofty spiritual qualities.

PLATE P. 224

It will be apparent that there are points of affinity here with the realistic Ethiopian heads of the 7th century B.C., but the differences between the two eras are equally marked.

In Egyptian art the sculpture of figures in the round was from the very beginning governed by certain laws. The figure was shown in direct full-face or in direct profile, embedded in a cube or a pillar. Thus a work of sculpture became a sum of individual parts, each one having an equal part to play, its form reflecting the artist's imagination and experience. In the course of the long history of Egyptian art there gradually evolved a sense of the organic links between the individual parts, a tendency towards realistic portraiture. But this element of realism never goes beyond the details; it is imposed from without upon the traditional forms. Thus even the realistic treatment of faces during the Ethiopian period is confined to the rendering of typical features: the figure is not conceived as a living whole, starting from its inner essence.

It is precisely this character that distinguishes the 'Green Head'. The realistic treatment of its external form stands in contrast to the astonishing, and essentially non-realistic, symmetry of the face, with its ornamental calligraphy of lines. Yet in spite of this contrast we have here a most impressive portrait — the portrait of an individual with a noble spiritual character. It might almost be the work of some Roman sculptor in the Republican era.

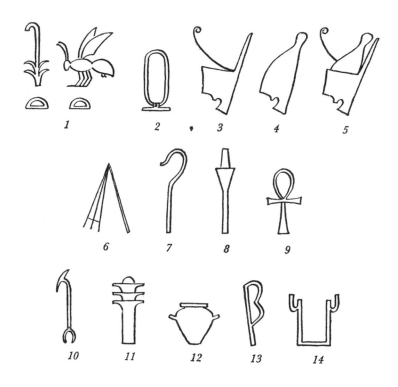

FIG. 79 — *Hieroglyphs with a purely pictographic significance, which occur frequently on figures or as amulets. Cf. p. 149.*

1. *King of Upper and Lower Egypt (nj-swt, bjtj)*
2. *Cartouche containing the name of the king*
3. *Crown of Lower Egypt*
4. *Crown of Upper Egypt*
5. *Double Crown*
6. *Scourge: attribute of gods and kings*
7. *Sceptre: attribute of gods and kings. Symbol for 'to rule' (heka)*
8. *Sceptre: symbol for power (sechem)*
9. *Symbol for life (anch)*
10. *Sceptre: hieroglyphic sign for well-being (was)*
11. *Eternity (djed)*
12. *Heart (ib)*
13. *Truth and Justice (maat)*
14. *Immortal substance (ka), roughly corresponding to our word 'soul'*

# NOTES

1 Two nilometers have survived up to the present day: one on Rhoda Island (Cairo), and the other on Elephantine Island (Aswan).

2 A. Scharff, *Die Altertümer der Vor- und Frühzeit Ägyptens,* Vol. 2 (Berlin, 1931), Fig. 25, Plates 13 and 59.

3 Small female figure from Abu Sir el Malaq, height 5.7 cm., in: A. Scharff, op. cit., Plates 15, 73.

4 Pyramid texts, Formula 257. A. Erman, *The Literature of the Ancient Egyptians,* translated by A. M. Blackman (London, 1927), pp. 4 f.

5 In the Louvre, Paris. *Journal of Egyptian Archaeology,* Vol. V, Pl. 32.

6 A. Scharff, *Handbuch der Archäologie,* I (Textband): *Die Denkmäler* (Munich, 1938), p. 462, Pl. 58 (i).

7 Limestone statue, measuring 2 metres in height, from Coptos where the god Min was worshipped. Now in the Ashmolean Museum, Oxford. H. Ranke, *Meisterwerke der ägyptischen Kunst* (Basle, 1948), Pl. 1.

8 From a New Kingdom papyrus, now in Leyden. A. Erman, *The Literature of the Ancient Egyptians,* translated by A. M. Blackman (London, 1927), pp. 92 f.

9 From the 'Dispute with his Soul of One who is tired of Life'. A. Erman, op. cit., pp. 86 f.

10 From A. Erman, op. cit. pp. 132 f.

11 From the 'Dispute with his Soul of One who is tired of Life' (see note 9).

12 The step mastaba tomb of King Zoser, usually referred to as a pyramid, is rectangular in plan, whereas the genuine pyramid is always square. The architectural concept of the Zoser tomb is based on the rectangular superstructure — mastaba — found on tombs already in the prehistoric period. These layers are placed one upon another, in decreasing size, thereby producing the impression of a pyramid.

13 A. Scharff, *Handbuch der Archäologie,* Vol. I: *Die Denkmäler* (Munich, 1938).

14 Mycerinus between two goddesses. A group of statues measuring 95 cm. in height, now in the Egyptian Museum, Cairo. Mycerinus and his wife: life-size group of statues in the Egyptian Museum, Cairo and the Museum of Fine Arts, Boston. C. Lange and M. Hirmer, *Egypt* (London, 1956), Pl. 44-47.

15 Wooden statue from Sakkara, now in the Egyptian Museum, Cairo. C. Lange and M. Hirmer, *Egypt* (London, 1956), Pl. 54.

16 From Hierakonpolis, now in the Egyptian Museum, Cairo. H. Schäfer and W. Andrae, *Die Kunst des Alten Orients* (Berlin, 1925), 3rd ed., p. 284.

[17] Recorded in a papyrus from the reign of Thutmosis III in St. Petersburg (Leningrad). A. Erman, op. cit., pp. 75 f.

[18] N. de G. Davies and A. H. Gardiner, *The Tomb of Antefoker* (London, 1920).

[19] P. E. Newberry, *Beni Hasan II* (London, 1893-1900), Pl. 5.

[20] In the Museum of Fine Arts, Boston. Dunham-Smith, 'A Middle Kingdom Painted Coffin from Deir el-Bahari', in: *Scritti in Onore di Ippolito Rosellini,* Vol. I (Pisa, 1949), pp. 263 ff.

[21] H. G. Evers, *Staat aus dem Stein,* Vol. I (Munich, 1929), Plates 26-30.

[22] H. G. Evers, op. cit., Plates 48-50 and Fig. 60.

[23] From the poems on Thebes and the god Amun in a papyrus from the reign of Ramses II, now in Leyden. A. Erman, op. cit., pp. 293 ff.

[24] Inscription in the tomb of Eye at Amarna. A. Erman, op. cit., pp. 288 f.

[25] Papyrus from the XXIInd Dynasty, now in Cairo. A. Erman. op. cit., pp. 234 f.

[26] E. Naville, *The Temple of Deir el-Bahari* (London, 1895-1908), Pts. I-VI.

[27] N. de G. Davies, *The Tomb of the Vizier Ramose* (London, 1941), Plates 29, 33.

[28] Granite statue from Karnak, measuring 1.10 m. in height, now in the Egyptian Museum, Cairo. E. Drioton, *L'art égyptien* (Paris, 1950), p. 78, Pl. 69.

[29] Brownish slate statuette, measuring 22 cm. in height, now in the Metropolitan Museum, New York. A. Scharff, op. cit., p. 573, Pl. 95 (i).

[30] Granite statue from Karnak, measuring 1.75 m. in height, now in the Egyptian Museum, Cairo. G. Legrain, *Statues et statuettes* (Cairo, 1914), Vol. III, Pl. 10.

I. EGYPT AND ADJOINING LANDS

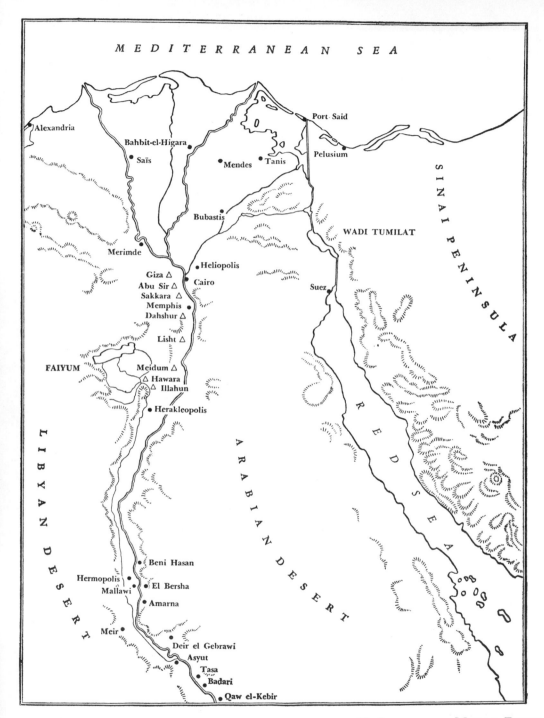

II. LOWER AND MIDDLE EGYPT

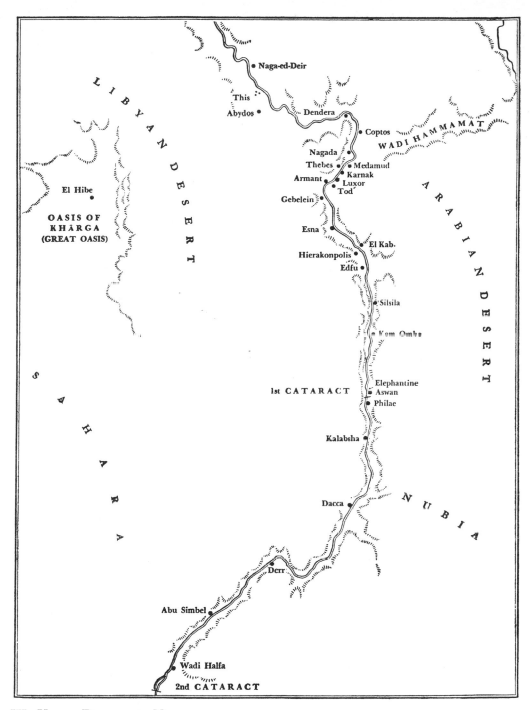

III. Upper Egypt and Nubia

## Egypt

| Rulers | History and Culture |
|---|---|

| | |
|---|---|
| 5000 B.C. | **PREHISTORIC ERA** New Stone Age (Neolithic) TASIAN AND MERIMDIAN CULTURES Settlement of Nile valley |
| 4000 | Stone and Copper Age (Chalcolithic) |

*Upper Egypt*        *Lower Egypt*

BADARIAN CULTURE     FAIYUMIC AND OMARIAN CULTURE
                                 NAGADA I CULTURE
                                 Burnished red clay vessels with white decoration. Cosmetic palettes.
                                 NAGADA II CULTURE (c. 3300) Yellowish-red clay vessels with brown decoration.

| | | |
|---|---|---|
| 3000 | | **ARCHAIC PERIOD** Formation of unified state under hegemony of Upper Egypt. Influence of Jamdat Nasr. Cosmetic palettes. Invention of hieroglyphic writing and calendar. Narmer palette. Beginnings of sculpture. Foundation of the city of Memphis. Royal tombs near Abydos and Memphis. Stone vessels. Copper in use. |
| | Ist and IInd DYNASTIES (c. 2950-2660) Thinites. King Narmer | |
| | IIIrd DYNASTY (c. 2660-2590) King Zoser et al. | **OLD KINGDOM** (Pyramid Period) Step Pyramid of King Zoser, near Sakkara. Reliefs and statues in tombs of officials. |
| 2500 | IVth DYNASTY (c. 2590-2470) Kings Cheops, Chephren, Mycerinus, et al. | Pyramids and mastaba necropolis at Giza. Bent Pyramid of King Snefru at Dahshur. |
| | Vth DYNASTY (c. 2470-2320) Kings Userkaf, Sahura, Niuserra, Unas, et al. | Sun cult. Pyramids and Sanctuary of the Sun near Abu Sir and Sakkara. Flowering period of reliefs and sculpture in sepulchral palaces of officials at Sakkara. |
| | VIth DYNASTY (c. 2320-2160) Kings Teti, Pepi I, II et al. | Collapse of state; power passes to nomarchs. Sepulchral palaces at Sakkara and nomarchs' tombs in Upper and Middle Egypt. |
| | VIIth and VIIIth DYNASTIES (c. 2160-2134) Many kings with short reigns | Dissolution of royal power and end of artistic tradition. |
| | IXth and Xth DYNASTIES (2134-c. 2040) Herakleopolitan rulers in Lower and Middle Egypt | **FIRST INTERMEDIATE PERIOD** Herakleopolitan rulers overlap chronologically with XIth Dynasty. |
| 2000 | XIth DYNASTY (2134-1991) Local princes at Thebes. Kings by the name of Mentuhotep | **MIDDLE KINGDOM** Re-unification of Egypt by Mentuhotep II. Capital at Thebes. Artistic renaissance in reliefs and sculpture. Mortuary temple at Deir el-Bahari, Thebes. |

| Mesopotamia — Iran<br>Asia Minor | Greece — Crete — Troy | Italy | |
|---|---|---|---|
| Neolithic | Neolithic | Neolithic | 5000<br>B.C. |
| TELL HALAF CULTURE<br>Samarra pottery<br>Pottery at Susa, Sialk, Hissar. | | | 4000 |
| AL 'UBAID CULTURE | | | |
| URUK PERIOD | | | |
| | | | 3000 |
| JAMDAT NASR PERIOD<br>First written records<br>Urban culture at Susa | | | |
| IST DYNASTY OF UR (SUMER) | | | |
| | Troy I<br>Early Minoan period on Crete.<br>Early Helladic period in Greece.<br>Pelos group in Cyclades.<br>Troy II | | 2500 |
| AKKADIAN DYNASTY<br>Sargon I (c. 2350)<br>Naram-Sin (2334-2297) | | | |
| Gudea of Lagash (2120) | Syros group in Cyclades. | | |
| King Ur-Nammu of Ur (2112) | Troy III-V | | |
| IIIRD DYNASTY OF UR<br>Palestine and Syria under<br>Egyptian rule. Immigration of<br>Hittites into northern Syria. | Immigration of Indo-European<br>Hittites to Anatolia. | | |
| EARLY ELAMITE PERIOD<br>Elamites destroy Babylon and<br>Ur. Phoenicia and Syria under<br>Egyptian rule. Babylonian he-<br>gemony in Mesopotamia.<br>DYNASTIES OF ISIN AND LARSA | Middle Minoan period on Crete.<br>Foundations laid of palaces.<br>*Kamares style.* | | 2000 |

## Egypt

| Rulers | History and Culture |
|---|---|
| **XIIth Dynasty** (c. 1991-1785) Kings by the name of Amenemhat and Sesostris | Memphis again royal residence. Pyramids in the Faiyum and at Dahshur. Faiyum brought into cultivation. Conquest of Nubia up to 2nd Cataract. Artistic flowering. Development of portraiture under Sesostris III and Amenemhat III. |
| **XIIIth Dynasty** (c. 1785-1660) Fifty rulers with brief reigns: Sebekhotep, Neferhotep, et al. | **SECOND INTERMEDIATE PERIOD** Disintegration of unified state and culture. No significant works of art. |
| **XIVth Dynasty** (c. 1785-1660) | Rules over Delta independently of simultaneous XIIIth Dynasty. |
| **XVth Dynasty** (c. 1660-1550) Asiatic Hyksos kings in Lower and Middle Egypt | **ALIEN RULE BY HYKSOS** |
| **XVIth Dynasty** (c. 1660-1550) Simultaneous rule by Asiatic and Egyptian kings | XVth and XVIth Dynasties ruling simultaneously |
| **XVIIth Dynasty** (c. 1600-1557) Local princes at Thebes | Rules simultaneously with XVth and XVIth Dynasties. The last king, Kamose, frees Egypt from alien rule. |
| **XVIIIth Dynasty** (1557-1304) Amenophis I (1532-1511) Thutmosis I and II (1511-1490) Thutmosis III (1490-1437) and Hatshepsut (1490-c. 1470, regent on behalf of Thutmosis III) | **NEW KINGDOM** Hyksos finally expelled by Amasis, brother of Kamose; country re-united under Theban rule. Campaigns to Syria and Nubia by Thutmosis III. Greatest expansion of kingdom. Construction of part of temple at Karnak. Mortuary Temple of Hatshepsut at Deir el-Bahari. *Austere style:* First phase of artistic development in New Kingdom. Tombs in Valley of the Kings in mountains on west bank at Thebes. *Mature style* |
| Amenophis II (1437-1410) Thutmosis IV (1410-1400) Amenophis III (1400-1362) | Amenophis III marries Tiy, a commoner. Construction of temple at Luxor. Refinement of taste and higher living standards. Flowering of craftsmanship. Invention of coloured enamel. |
| Amenophis IV-Akhnaton (1363-1346) | Transfer of royal residence to Amarna. Cult of Aton. Loss of possessions in Asia. *Amarna art: expressive style.* |
| Tutankhamun and Eye (1346-1334) Horemheb (1334-1304) | Seat of government moved back to Thebes. Age of Restoration. In art: echoes of a more spiritual Amarna style. |

B.C.
1900

1700

1600

1500

1400

| Mesopotamia — Iran<br>Asia Minor | Greece — Crete — Troy | Italy | |
|---|---|---|---|
| | Middle Helladic period in<br>Greece.<br>Troy VI | | |
| EARLY BABYLONIAN PERIOD<br>(c. 1900-1600) | | | B.C.<br>1900 |
| Hammurabi of Babylon<br>(1793-1750)<br>Phoenicians invent the<br>alphabet<br>Indo-European tribes invade<br>Persia. Hittite king Hattusil. | | | |
| | | | 1700 |
| | | | 1600 |
| | Late Helladic period in Greece. | | |
| Babylonia destroyed by<br>Hittite king Mursilis.<br>Kassites (c. 1600-1150)<br>Mitanni (c. 1600-1350) | Late Minoan period in Crete.<br>Cities founded. | | |
| | Gold masks from Mycenaean<br>tombs.<br>Flowering of Mycenaean culture. | | |
| MIDDLE ELAMITE PERIOD (Iran)<br>MIDDLE ASSYRIAN PERIOD<br>(Mesopotamia)<br>Kassites occupy Babylon.<br>Campaigns by Thutmosis III<br>to Syria. | Age of the citadels. | | 1500 |
| | Destruction of Palace<br>of Knossos. | | |
| Babylonia under Kassite rule. | | | 1400 |
| Kingdom of Mitanni<br>conquered by Hittites.<br><br>Assyrian kingdom wins<br>independence under<br>Assur-uballit | | | |

Egypt

| Rulers | History and Culture |
|---|---|
| **B.C.** | |
| **1300** XIXth Dynasty, Ramessids (1304-1200) Rasmes I, Seti I | Restoration of Egyptian rule over Palestine. Royal residence in eastern Delta. Architecture: temple at Abydos, columned hall in t at Karnak. |
| Ramses II Merneptah and Seti II | War against Hittites. Architecture: work on Luxo ple, Hypostyle Hall in temple at Karnak, rock-cut t at Abu Simbel. |
| **1200** XXth Dynasty, Ramessids (c. 1200-1185) Setnakht Ramses III (1198-1167) Ramses IV-XI | Battle with Peoples of the Sea. Temple at Medinet I |
| **1100** XXIst Dynasty (c. 1185-950) in Tanis: Smendes, Psusennes, Amenemopet | Smendes in Delta. |
| **1000** in Thebes: rule by priests | 'Theocracy of Amun' under High Priests Herihor, Pinujem, et al. |
| XXIInd Dynasty (from 950 Libyans) Kings of Libyan origin, from military aristocracy | Residence at Bubastis |
| XXIIIrd Dynasty (to 730) Kings Sheshonk, Osorkon, Takeloth and Petubastis | Lesser branch of XXIInd Dynasty. Rules simultane in Middle and Upper Egypt. Perfectioning of bronze-casting. |
| XXIVth Dynasty (c. 730-712) Kings Tefnakht and Bocchoris | Dynasty from Saïs in Delta. |
| XXVth Dynasty (c. 750/712-655) Kings Piankhi, Shabaka, Shebitku, Taharka, Tanutamun | Ethiopian kings from Napata at 4th Cataract claim E tian throne as worshippers of Amun. Ethiopian j cesses rule as 'Divine Wives' of Amun. Sacerdotal j cess in Thebes. Flowering of the arts, especially por heads. Assyrian invasion of Lower Egypt. Sack of Th (671—663). |
| XXVIth Dynasty (664-525) 'Saites', Kings Psammetichus I-III, Necho, Apries, Amasis | Royal residence at Saïs in Delta. Opulent flowerin the arts, especially bronze and stone sculpture. |

| Mesopotamia — Iran<br>Asia Minor | Greece — Crete — Troy | Italy | |
|---|---|---|---|
| | Troy VII | | B.C.<br>1300 |
| Southern Syria occupied by Seti I. Battle of Kadesh.<br>King Untashgal (c. 1234-1227) | | | |
| Invasion by Peoples of the Sea. Hittite Kingdom destroyed. | Destruction of Mycenaean citadels. | | 1200 |
| Babylon conquered by Tiglath-pileser I of Assyria. Assyrian power extended northwards. Foundation of Syrian-Hittite states in northern Syria | Dorian Migration<br><br>*Sub-Minoan art*<br>*Sub-Mycenaean art* | Etruscans migrate into central Italy<br>Beginning of Villanova culture | 1100 |
| | Colonisation in Mediterranean<br>*Protogeometric art* | | 1000 |
| Aramean invasions. End of old Assyrian Empire. Babylon again becomes independent.<br>King Solomon (963-925)<br>Revival of Syria.<br>Shalmaneser III (859-827)<br>Cimmerian invasion from Caucasus.<br>Late Elamite period in Iran. | Beginning of Homeric epics | Foundation of Rome' according to Roman annals (753)<br>Rome under the kings | |
| Sargon II (722-705)<br>Sennacherib (705-681)<br>Babylon destroyed by Sennacherib (698). | Transition from wooden to stone architecture in Greece<br>*Archaic art* | | |
| Achaemenes (700-675) founds Achaemenid empire in Persia<br><br>Assur: Esarhaddon (681-668)<br>Assur-bani-pal (668-626) | Development of monumental sculpture in the round in Greece<br>Constitution of Solon in Athens (593) | Earliest tumulus graves at Caere (Cerveteri) | |
| Scythian invasions. Assur conquered by Chaldeans and Medes (612).<br>Circa 600: Persia a world power (Achaemenids).<br>Mesopotamia becomes a Persian province. | Peisistratus makes himself tyrant of Athens (560) | | |

243

## Egypt

| Rulers | History and Culture |
|--------|---------------------|
| **B.C.**<br>**500**<br>XXVIIth Dynasty (525-504)<br>'Persians' | Cambyses conquers Egypt and turns it into a Persian satrapy. Canal built from Nile to Red Sea. |
| XXVIIIth and XXIXth Dynasties (504-380)<br>Kings Amyrtaeus, Nepherites, Achoris | From Mendes in the Delta. |
| XXXth Dynasty (380-343)<br>Kings Nectanebo I, Teos, Nectanebo II | From Sebennythos in the Delta. New flowering period in art, esp. sculpture.<br><br>Egypt again a Persian province (343-332).<br><br>Alexander the Great conquers Egypt (332). Foundation of Alexandria. Spread of Hellenic art.<br><br>Struggle between the Diadochi (323-304). |
| Ptolemaic Rule (304-30)<br>Ptolemy I-XV<br>Cleopatra (51-30 B.C.) | PTOLEMAIC PERIOD<br><br>Cleopatra defeated by Augustus.<br>Egypt becomes Roman province. |
| **0**<br><br>**100**<br>**A.D.** | Domitian encourages cult of Isis and Serapis in Italy.<br><br>Hadrian founds Antinoë in memory of his friend Antinous, drowned in the Nile.<br>Founding of Christian (Coptic) communities in Egypt. |
| **200**<br><br>**300** | Roman Empire partitioned between Rome and Byzantium (395) |

| Mesopotamia — Iran Asia Minor | Greece — Crete — Troy | Italy | |
|---|---|---|---|
| Nebuchadnezzar II (597-587) subjugates Judaea. Israelite captivity in Babylon. Darius I (522-486) Xerxes (486-465) Asia Minor becomes Persian province. | Persian Wars | Collapse of Etruscan monarchy in Rome (509). Roman Republic | B.C. 500 |
| Circa 500: Rebellion by Ionians in Asia Minor against Persian rule. Persian Wars (to 448). | *Classical Greek art* Pericles Peloponnesian War | | |
| Peace of Antalcidas (387). Persia obtains sovereignty over the Greek cities in Asia Minor and Cyprus. | The Thirty Tyrants in Athens | Rome taken by Celts | |
| | *Hellenism* | Rebellion of Latins and Campani against Rome | |
| Conquests of Alexander the Great. | Alexander the Great | | |
| Seleucid Empire in Mesopotamia and Iran. | Rule of Diadochi | | |
| Parthian Empire in Mesopotamia and Iran. Parthian conquest of Babylon and Assyria. Jerusalem destroyed by Titus (70 A.D.) | Corinth destroyed by Romans Greece a Roman province | Punic Wars Destruction of Carthage and Corinth Julius Caesar Augustus founds Roman Empire | 0 |
| Mesopotamia becomes Roman province. | | | 100 A.D. |
| Sassanid Empire in Iran. | | Constantine the Great | 200 |
| | Byzantine Empire | Diarchy of sons of Constantine | 300 |

# BIBLIOGRAPHY

## GENERAL WORKS

*Baedeker, K.,* Egypt. 8th ed. Leipzig, 1929.
*Kees, H.,* Das alte Ägypten: eine kleine Landeskunde. Berlin, 1955.
*Kusch, E.,* Ägypten im Bild. Munich, 1955.
*Lange, K.,* Ägypten: Landschaft und Kunst. Berlin, 1943.
*Mekhitarian, A.,* Introduction à l'Égypte. Brussels, 1956.
*Posener, G.,* A Dictionary of Egyptian Civilization. Translated by A. Macfarlane. London, 1962.
*Ziock, H.,* Ägypten. Kurt Schroeder, Reiseführer. Bonn, 1955.

## HISTORY

*Breasted, J. H.,* A History of Egypt. London, 1950.
*Meyer, E.,* Geschichte des Altertums, vols. 1—3. Stuttgart-Berlin, 1925—37.
*Otto, E.,* Ägypten: der Weg des Pharaonenreiches. Stuttgart, 1953.
*Scharff, A. and Moortgat, A.,* Ägypten und Vorderasien im Altertum. Munich, 1950.

## HISTORY OF CULTURE AND IDEAS

*Erman, A. and Ranke, H.,* Ägypten und ägyptisches Leben im Altertum. Tübingen, 1923.
*Frankfort, H. and H. A., Wilson, J. A., Jacobsen, Th., and Irwin, W. A.,* The Intellectual Adventure of Ancient Man: an Essay on Speculative Thought in the Ancient Near East. Chicago, 1946.
*Kees, H.,* Ägypten: Kulturgeschichte des Alten Orients, I, in: Handbuch der Altertumswissenschaft, Section III, Part I, 3 vols. Munich, 1933.
*Spiegel, J.,* Das Werden der altägyptischen Hochkultur. Glückstadt, 1935.
*Wolf, W.,* Die Welt der Ägypter. Stuttgart, 1955.
*Wreszinski, W.,* Atlas zur altägyptischen Kulturgeschichte. Parts I-III. Leipzig, 1923-38.

## RELIGION

*Bonnet, H.,* Reallexikon der altägyptischen Religionsgeschichte. Berlin, 1952.
*Drioton, E.,* La religion égyptienne, in: Histoire des religions, vol. 3. Paris, 1955.
*Erman, A.,* Die Religion der Ägypter. Berlin, 1934.

*Frankfort, H. A.,* Ancient Egyptian Religion. New York, 1948.
*Junker, H.,* Pyramidenzeit: das Wesen der ägyptischen Religion. Zurich-Cologne, 1949.
*Kees, H.,* Ägypten, in: Religionsgeschichtliches Lesebuch, ed. by Bertholet, 2nd ed. Tübingen, 1928.
*Kees, H.,* Der Götterglaube im Alten Ägypten, 2nd ed. Berlin, 1956.
*Kees, H.,* Totenglaube und Jenseitsvorstellungen der Alten Ägypter, 2nd ed. Berlin, 1956.
*Roeder, G.,* Volksglaube im Pharaonenreich. Stuttgart, 1952.

## PHILOLOGY

*Edel, E.,* Altägyptische Grammatik, I. Rome, 1955.
*Erman, A.,* Die Hieroglyphen, 2nd ed. Berlin-Leipzig, 1923.
*Erman, A.,* Ägyptische Grammatik, 4th ed. Berlin, 1928.
*Erman, A.,* Neuägyptische Grammatik, 2nd ed. Leipzig, 1933.
*Erman, A. and Grapow, H.,* Wörterbuch der ägyptischen Sprache, vols. 1-6 (and authorities, vols. 1-5). Leipzig, 1926-55.
*Schott, S.,* Hieroglyphen: Untersuchungen zum Ursprung der Schrift. Wiesbaden, 1951.

## LITERATURE

*Bissing, F. W. von,* Altägyptische Lebensweisheit. Zurich, 1955.
*Erman, A.,* The Literature of the Ancient Egyptians. Tr. by A. M. Blackman. London, 1927.
*Pieper, M.,* Die altägyptische Literatur. Potsdam, 1927.
*Scharff, A.,* Ägyptische Sonnenlieder. Berlin, 1922.
*Schott, S.,* Altägyptische Liebeslieder. Zurich, 1950.

## ART IN GENERAL

*Anthes, R.,* Ägyptische Plastik in Meisterwerken. Stuttgart, 1954.
*Bissing, F. W. von,* Denkmäler ägyptischer Skulptur. Munich, 1911-4.
*Champdor, A.,* L'Égypte des pharaons. (Fr. & Eng.) Paris, 1955.
*Desroches-Noblecourt, C.,* Le style égyptien. Paris, 1946.

Drioton, E., L'art égyptien. Paris, 1950.

Edwards, I. E. S., The Pyramids of Egypt. London, 1947.

Hamann, R., Ägyptische Kunst. Berlin, 1944.

Hermann, A. and Schwan, W., Ägyptische Kleinkunst. Berlin, 1940.

Hornemann, B., Types of Ancient Egyptian Statuary, vols. I-III. Copenhagen, 1951-7.

Lange, K., Ägyptische Kunst. Zurich-Berlin, 1943.

Lange, K., Lebensbilder aus der Pharaonenzeit: Meisterwerke altägyptischer Reliefkunst und Malerei. Berlin, 1952.

Lange, K. and Hirmer, M., Egypt. Translated by R. H. Boothroyd. London, 1956.

Legrain, G., Statues et statuettes de rois et des particuliers. Cairo, 1914.

Mekhitarian, A., Die ägyptische Malerei. Geneva, 1954.

Müller, H. W., Ägyptische Malerei. Berlin, 1959.

Ranke, H., Meisterwerke der ägyptischen Kunst. Basle, 1948.

Schäfer, H., Die Kunst Ägyptens. Propyläen-Kunstgeschichte, Die Kunst des Alten Orients 3rd ed. Berlin, 1925.

Scharff, A., Handbuch der Archäologie, I. Textband: Die Denkmäler. Munich, 1938.

Steindorff, G., Die Kunst der Ägypter. Leipzig, 1928.

UNESCO World Art Series. Egypt: Paintings from Tombs and Temples. Introd. by J. Vandier. Paris, 1954.

Wolf, W., Die Kunst Ägyptens. Stuttgart, 1957.

## PREHISTORIC AND ARCHAIC PERIODS

Capart, J., Primitive Art in Egypt. London, 1905.

Petrie, Sir William M. F., Prehistoric Egypt. London, 1920.

Roeder, G., Die vorgeschichtliche Plastik Ägyptens in ihrer Bedeutung für die Bildung des ägyptischen Stils. Ipek, 1926.

Scharff, A., Grundzüge der ägyptischen Vorgeschichte. Morgenland, No. 12. Leipzig, 1927.

Scharff, A., Die Altertümer der Vor- und Frühzeit Ägyptens. Berlin, 1929-31.

Vandier, J., Manuel d'archéologie égyptienne, I: les époques de formation. Paris, 1952.

## OLD KINGDOM

Aldred, C., Old Kingdom Art in Ancient Egypt. London, 1949.

Junker, G., Giza. Vols. 1-12. Vienna, 1929-55.

Klebs, L., Die Reliefs des Alten Reiches. Heidelberg, 1925.

Reisner, G., A History of the Giza Necropolis. 2 vols. Cambridge, 1942, 1954.

Selim Hasan, Excavations at Giza. Vols. 1-8. Oxford-Cairo, 1932-53.

Smith, W. St., A History of Egyptian Sculpture and Painting in the Old Kingdom. 2nd ed. London, 1949.

## MIDDLE KINGDOM

Aldred, C., Middle Kingdom Art in Ancient Egypt. London, 1950.

Davies, N. de G. and Gardiner, A. H., The Tomb of Antefoker. London, 1920.

Evers, H. G., Staat aus dem Stein. Munich, 1929.

Klebs, L., Die Reliefs und Malereien des Mittleren Reiches. Heidelberg, 1925.

Lange, K., Sesostris. Munich, 1954.

Newberry, P. E., Beni Hasan II. London, 1893-1900.

## NEW KINGDOM

Aldred, C., New Kingdom Art in Ancient Egypt. London, 1951.

Davies, N. de G., The Tomb of the Vizier Ramose. London, 1941.

Klebs, L., Die Reliefs und Malereien des Neuen Reiches, I. Heidelberg, 1934.

Steindorff, G., Die Blütezeit des Pharaonenreiches. 2nd ed. Bielefeld-Leipzig, 1926.

## LATE PERIOD

Bosse, K., Die menschliche Figur in der Rundplastik der ägyptischen Spätzeit von der XXII. bis zur XXX. Dynastie. Glückstadt, 1936.

# GLOSSARY

**basalt**
Ore-bearing rock of igneous origin, belonging to the basic sub-division. Varies in composition and colouring.

**block-statue**
Carved figure of a squatting human being, which has the general shape of a cube. Only the head, hands and occasionally the feet are worked in such a way that they remain outside the cubic shape. From the Middle Kingdom onwards this was the usual type of statue erected in temples to represent high-ranking officials and priests.

**breccia**
Rock in which minerals and fossils are embedded.

**Bubastide dynasty**
Libyan ruling family of the XXIInd Dynasty, named after the royal residence at Bubastis, in the Delta.

**canopic jars**
Jars in which the viscera of the deceased are interred.

**cartouche**
Oval frame enclosing the name of a king.

**Delta**
Fertile alluvial land at the mouth of the Nile.

**diorite**
Greyish-green plutonic rock.

**electrum**
Argentiferous gold.

**fetish**
Any object thought to possess special power or to be the abode of spirits.

**funerary art**
Reliefs and murals executed in sepulchral chambers, and also statues erected in tombs. Their motifs and style are determined by the magic or religious function which, according to Egyptian beliefs, they fulfil.

**funerary texts**
To ensure that the deceased enjoys a life beyond the grave he is provided with funerary gifts and pictorial representations, as well as formulae written on the walls of his tomb or on papyri placed in the sarcophagus. These written invocations are intended to protect the deceased from all danger. Best known of all are the pyramid texts of the Old Kingdom, the coffin texts and the Book of the Dead in the Middle Kingdom, and the guides to the world beyond in the New Kingdom.

**Hall of Annals**
Hall built by Thutmosis III in the temple at Karnak, on the walls there is an exact account of his campaigns and the loot obtained.

**Hathor column**
Column bearing, on all four sides of the capital, the head of the goddess Hathor.

**idol**
Image of a supernatural and divine power.

**jubilee cloak**
Ceremonial garment used in enthronement ceremonies and to celebrate royal jubilees.

**jubilee temple**
Small temple used for the ceremony of the royal jubilee.

**ka**
Immortal human substance, approximately corresponding to the concept of 'soul'.

**Kush**
Egyptian term for Nubia (Ethiopia). The governor responsible for the administration of this province is called 'the King's son of Kush'.

**local gods**
Gods worshipped within a limited area, such as a town or nome.

**magic**
Belief in forces which have no apparent natural cause and are thought peculiar to the gods. The believer in magic, as distinct from the religious believer, seeks to conjure up these forces by means of representations and inscriptions, and thereby to enforce wishes that it is beyond human ability to fulfil. Instead of prayer and submission to divine laws there is belief in the power of invocation, made effective by some formula.

**mastaba**
(Arabic: bench). Built-up superstructure of a tomb, rectangular in plan, with sloping walls.

**monoliths**
Large architectural members (pillars) consisting of single block of stone.

**mummification**
According to Egyptian belief life after death depended on preservation of the body. Soon

after the beginning of the historic era mummified bodies are found. The viscera were removed and interred separately; the skin was prepared with a solution of salt and natron; then the body was wrapped in sheets of linen impregnated with resin or stucco, in which the features of the deceased were modelled. Later a hard covering of linen and stucco was placed around the body, the form and colour of which reproduced the features of the deceased. This developed into a mummy coffin.

*myth*
Fictitious narrative in which the realm of the gods and the mystery of creation are interpreted in accordance with human concepts.

*naos bearers*
Statues of standing or kneeling priests and officials holding a shrine or chapel containing idols. From the New Kingdom onwards, and especially during the Late Period, they frequently appear as statues in temples.

*obsidian*
Natural volcanic glass.

*offering-room*
The chamber of the tomb in which the priests and relatives of the deceased make sacrificial offerings and recite prayers.

*Osiride pillar*
Statue in the shape of the god of the dead, Osiris, depicted leaning against a pillar, in a close-fitting mummy-swathing, holding a scourge and sceptre.

*porphyry*
Reddish rock of volcanic origin containing sprinklings of crystalline minerals.

*private sculpture*
Figures in the round of members of the privileged classes.

*private tombs*
Tombs of members of the privileged classes, as distinct from those of kings. The style of official royal monuments is often very different from that of monuments commissioned by private individuals, so that it is worth making a distinction between them.

*pylon*
Fortress-like monumental gateway to a temple.

*pyramid*
Tomb of Egyptian kings in the Old and Middle Kingdom. The body of the deceased ruler is laid to rest in an inaccessible chamber.

*Saites*
Family of princes of the XXVIth Dynasty, from the town of Saïs in the Delta.

*satrapy*
Province.

*scarabaeus (scarab)*
Dung beetle. In this form the Egyptians worshipped the rising sun. As a hieroglyph it denotes 'to become', 'to come into being'. Scarabs, worked in different materials, and bearing incised symbols, names, and figures, serve as seals or amulets. Large scarabs — so-called heart-scarabs — were inserted into the bandages during the mummification.

*serdab*
Statue-chamber in a tomb, in which the funerary statue of the deceased was erected.

*shaduf*
Device for raising water, with two levers and a leather bucket (or plaited basket), used for irrigation.

*Sothis*
Sirius (constellation).

*sphinx*
Body of a lion with the head of a king. Symbolic of the king's strength.

*stele*
Upright slab bearing inscriptions and figures, serving as a tombstone or boundary mark.

*syncretism*
Overlapping and coincidence of meaning (applied to objects with characteristics formerly ascribed only to one of them). During the Late Period in Egypt, this term is used to denote a blurring of the distinct qualities previously ascribed to the various gods.

*temple art*
Figures in relief and in the round representing gods and kings, expressing the link between the pharaoh and the gods. During the Ramessid period these are supplemented by historical scenes on the external walls of temples, and from the New Kingdom onwards, often by statues of officials and priests.

*Thinites*
Princely family of the Ist and IInd Dynasties, from the town of This.

*uraeus*
Snake. Tutelary goddess of Lower Egypt. An attribute of gods and kings, it appears in conjunction with the royal head-dress.

*vizier*
The most senior state official, responsible for the administration of a district.

# INDEX

*The numerals in italics refer to the plates and figures. The letter (G) indicates Glossary.*